STREET ITALIAN 2

The Best of Naughty Italian

DAVID BURKE

John Wiley & Sons, Inc.

New York • Chichester • Weinheim • Brisbane • Singapore • Toronto

Design and Production: David Burke
Copy Editor and Translator: Alessio Filippi
Front Cover Illustration: Ty Semaka
Inside Illustrations: Ty Semaka
Photography: Rick Olson

This book is printed on acid-free paper. ∞

Published by John Wiley & Sons, Inc.
Published simultaneously in Canada

This publication is designed to provide accurate and authoritative
information in regard to the subject matter covered. It is sold with the
understanding that the publisher is not engaged in rendering professional
services. If professional advice or other expert assistance is required, the
services of a competent professional person should be sought.

ISBN 0-471-38439-9

Printed in the United States of America

10 9 8 7 6 5 4 3 2 1

This book is dedicated to my family

CONTENTS

LESSON 1	DATING SLANG	9

Massimo mi ha tirato un bidone!

Massimo stood me up!

LESSON 2	NONVULGAR INSULTS & PUTDOWNS	23

Tipi come lui mi rompono le scatole!

Guys like him tick me off!

LESSON 3	VULGAR INSULTS AND NAME-CALLING	37

Accidenti alla quella gran porca di tua madre!

Screw you!

ACKNOWLEDGMENTS

I'm forever grateful to Alessio Filippi for his extraordinary contribution to this book. His insight into the spoken Italian language had me constantly amazed. He will always have my deepest appreciation and regard.

To say that Ty Semaka's illustrations are brilliant, hilarious, amazing, and magical would be an understatement. I consider myself so lucky to have found so much talent all wrapped up in one person.

I consider myself very fortunate to have been under the wing of so many wonderful people during the creation of this book. A tremendous and warm thanks goes to my pals at John Wiley & Sons: Chip Rossetti, Gerry Helferich, and Marcia Samuels. They are without a doubt the most friendly, supportive, encouraging, and infinitely talented group of people with which I've had the pleasure to work.

INTRODUCTION

You may be asking yourself, "What purpose could a book about Italian obscenities possibly serve other than simply to create shock value by listing gratuitous vulgar words and expressions?" There are three simple answers: (1) to avoid embarrassment; (2) to understand fully a conversation between native speakers; and (3) survival.

Although many teachers would prefer not to acknowledge this fact, obscenities are a living part of everyday Italian. They are used in movies, books, television and radio shows, newspapers, news broadcasts, magazines, to name a few categories.

Those who are not completely familiar with the Italian language often find themselves in awkward or embarrassing situations by using a word in such a way as to create a double meaning or a sexual innuendo.

STREET ITALIAN 2 is the first step-by-step guide of its kind to explore the most common expletives and obscenities used throughout Italy. This knowledge is an essential tool in self-defense for nonnative speakers as well as an entertaining guide for native speakers who may not be aware of how colorful the Italian language truly is.

STREET ITALIAN 2 is designed to teach the essentials of naughty Italian in ten lessons that are divided into five primary parts:

■ **DIALOGUE**

In this section, slang words *(shown in boldface)* are presented in an Italian dialogue on the left-hand page. A translation of the dialogue appears on the opposite page. On the following page, you'll find a *literal* translation of the dialogue that often proves to be hilarious!

■ **VOCABULARY**

This section spotlights all of the slang terms that were used in the dialogue and offers:

✔ an example of usage for each entry

✔ an English translation of the example

✔ synonyms, antonyms, variations, or special notes to give you a complete sense of the word or expression.

■ PRACTICE THE VOCABULARY

These word games and drills include all of the slang terms and idioms previously learned and will help you test yourself on your comprehension. *(The pages providing the answers to the drills are indicated at the beginning of this section.)*

■ DICTATION

This section will allow you to test yourself on your listening comprehension. If you are following along with your cassette, you will hear a series of sentences from the opening dialogue. These sentences will be read by a native speaker at normal conversational speed. When the sentences are read again, there will be a pause after each to give you time to write down what you have heard.

■ REVIEW

Following each sequence of five chapters is a summary review encompassing all the words and expressions learned up to that point.

■ GESTURES

What's Italian without gestures?! This section demonstrates some of the most common and colorful Italian gestures to help you indicate everything from love to rage.

The secret to learning **STREET ITALIAN 2** is to follow this simple checklist:

■ Make sure that you have a good grasp on each section before proceeding to the drills. If you've made more than two errors in a particular drill, simply go back and review...then try again!

■   *Remember:* This is a self-paced book, so take your time. You're not fighting the clock!

■   It's very important that you feel comfortable with each chapter before proceeding to the next. Words you've learned along the way may crop up in the following dialogues. So feel comfortable before moving on!

■   Make sure that you read the dialogues and drills aloud. This is an excellent way to become comfortable speaking colloquially and to begin thinking like a native.

IMPORTANT: Slang and obscenities must always be used with discretion. You certainly should not practice them with formal dignitaries or employers whom you are trying to impress! Most important, since a nonnative speaker of Italian may tend to sound forced or artificial using slang, your first goal should be to *recognize and understand* these types of words.

LEGEND

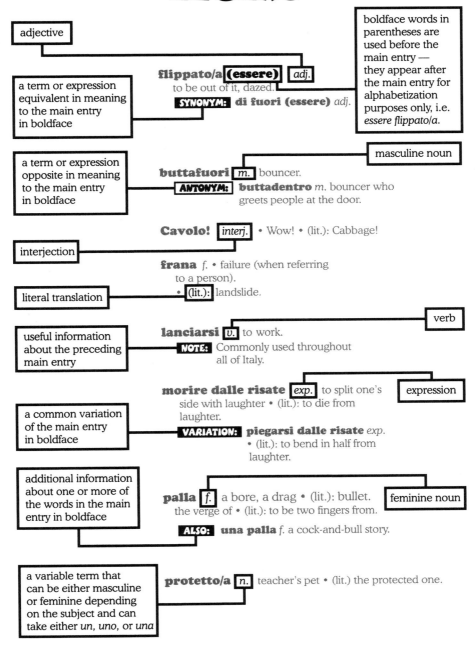

adjective

boldface words in parentheses are used before the main entry — they appear after the main entry for alphabetization purposes only, i.e. *essere flippato/a.*

flippato/a (essere) *adj.*
to be out of it, dazed.
SYNONYM: di fuori (essere) *adj.*

a term or expression equivalent in meaning to the main entry in boldface

masculine noun

a term or expression opposite in meaning to the main entry in boldface

buttafuori *m.* bouncer.
ANTONYM: buttadentro *m.* bouncer who greets people at the door.

Cavolo! *interj.* • Wow! • (lit.): Cabbage!

interjection

frana *f.* • failure (when referring to a person).
• (lit.): landslide.

literal translation

verb

useful information about the preceding main entry

lanciarsi *v.* to work.
NOTE: Commonly used throughout all of Italy.

morire dalle risate *exp.* to split one's side with laughter • (lit.): to die from laughter.
VARIATION: piegarsi dalle risate *exp.* • (lit.): to bend in half from laughter.

expression

a common variation of the main entry in boldface

additional information about one or more of the words in the main entry in boldface

palla *f.* a bore, a drag • (lit.): bullet.
the verge of • (lit.): to be two fingers from.
ALSO: una palla *f.* a cock-and-bull story.

feminine noun

a variable term that can be either masculine or feminine depending on the subject and can take either *un, uno,* or *una*

protetto/a *n.* teacher's pet • (lit.) the protected one.

5

STREET ITALIAN 2

PART 1

NAUGHTY ITALIAN

Massimo mi ha tirato un bidone!

(trans.): Massimo **stood me up**!
(lit.): Massimo **threw a trash can at me**!

Patrizia: Non riesco a crederci! Massimo, il **bellone** che ho conosciuto la scorsa settimana, mi **ha tirato un bidone**! Non faccio che conoscere dei gran **cazzoni** in giro.

Federica: Eh, gli uomini! A tutti piace **fare il galletto**. Credo che siano tutti dei **donnaioli** e che tutti **abbiano quel chiodo fisso in testa**. Ogni volta che vedono una bella **fighetta**, cercano di **beccarla** e danno per scontato che sia una **scopata facile**. Non appena però pensano che tu voglia **metterti seriamente con loro**, loro ti **mollano**!

Patrizia: Ed io poi sono così stanca di incontrare **vecchi sporcaccioni** che pensano che sia **amore a prima vista** dopo cinque minuti.

Federica: Mi è proprio successo la settimana scorsa! Ma penso che quello volesse soltanto far sesso; per cui gli ho detto di **levarsi di torno** e di andare invece a vedersi un bel **pornazzo**.

Massimo *stood me up!*

Patrizia: I can't believe this! Massimo, the **hunk** I met last week, **stood me up**! All I ever meet everywhere are big **jerks**.

Federica: Men! They all love to **flirt**. I think they're all **playboys** and all **have sex on the brain**. Every time they see a hot **chick**, they try to **pick her up** and assume she's an **easy lay**. But as soon as they think you want to **tie the knot**, they **dump you**!

Patrizia: And I'm so tired of meeting **dirty old men** who are convinced that it's **love at first sight** within five minutes.

Federica: That happened to me last week! But I think all he wanted was just sex. So I just told him to **beat it** and go see **an X-rated movie** instead.

Massimo *threw a trash can at me!*

Patrizia: I can't believe this! Massimo, the **attractive, but often stupid man** that I met last week, **threw a trash can at me**! All I ever meet around are big **dicks**.

Federica: Men! They all **do the rooster**. I think they're all **womanizers** and all **have that same nail fixed in their head**. Every time they see a hot **little vagina**, they try to **peck her** and assume she's an **easy sweep**. But as soon as they think you want to **put yourself with them**, they **release you**!

Patrizia: And I'm so tired of meeting **dirty old men** who are convinced that it's **love at first sight** within five minutes.

Federica: That happened to me last week! But I think all he wanted was just sex. So I just told him to **move from around** and go see a **porno** instead.

VOCABULARY

amore a prima vista *exp.* love at first sight.

> *example:* Lorenzo e Cecilia si sono incontrati recentemente ad una festa di Carnevale. Si sono parlati per alcuni minuti e si sono scambiati i loro numeri di telefono. È stato **amore a prima vista**!

> *translation:* Lorenzo and Cecilia met recently at a carnival party. They talked for a few minutes and exchanged phone numbers. It was **love at first sight**!

> **SYNONYM:** **un colpo di fulmine** *exp.* • (lit.): a thunderbolt (of love).

avere un chiodo fisso in testa *exp.* to be fixated on something • (lit.): to have a nail fixed in the head.

> *example:* Giorgio pensa ad Elena giorno e notte. Lui ha davvero un **chiodo fisso in testa**.

> *translation:* Giorgio thinks about Elena day and night. He's truly **fixated on her**.

beccare qualcuno *v.* to hit on someone, to pick someone up • (lit.): to peck.

> *example:* Ieri sera sono andato in un locale e ho **beccato** un' incredibile ragazza scandinava che sedeva al tavolo accanto al mio.

> *translation:* Last night, I went to a bar and **picked up** an incredible Scandinavian girl who sat at the table next to mine.

> **NOTE:** **locale** *m.* club or night club.

bellone *m.* a hunk, a man who is very good-looking yet stuck up.

     example: Ieri sera sono stata ad una festa con dei miei amici e ho conosciuto un gran **bellone** che si chiama Alessandro.

     translation: Last night, I went to a party with some friends and met a big **hunk** named Alessandro.

     NOTE: This comes from the masculine noun *fico*, meaning "a good-looking, attractive, and well built young man who wears trendy clothes."

     SYNONYM 1: **fichetto** *n.*

     SYNONYM 2: **figo della Madonna** *exp.*

     SYNONYM 3: **figone** *n.*

cazzone *m.* jerk, ass hole • (lit.): big "dick."

     example: Il tipo che ho conosciuto alla cena di Giovanni era un gran **cazzone**! Ha cercato di abbracciare e baciare tutte le ragazze carine che erano lì.

     translation: The guy I met at Giovanni's dinner party was a real **jerk**! He tried to hug and kiss all the cute girls who were there.

     SYNONYM: **stronzo** *n.* • (lit.): turd.

donnaiolo *m.* womanizer, someone who chases women, a playboy.

     example: Enrico non fa altro che guardare le ragazze! Che **donnaiolo**! Ieri sera, al locale, ha offerto da bere a tutte le ragazze che ha conosciuto!

     translation: Enrico does nothing but look at girls! What a **playboy**! Last night at the club, he bought drinks for all the girls he met!

     NOTE: This comes from *donna*, meaning "woman."

fare il galletto *exp.* to flirt • (lit.): to do like the rooster.

     example: Sabato sera, in discoteca, un ragazzo italiano ha **fatto il galletto** con me tutta la sera.

     translation: Saturday night at the dance club, an Italian guy **flirted** with me all night.

     SYNONYM 1: **flirtare** *v.* (from English).

     SYNONYM 2: **provarci** *v.* (lit.): to give it a try.

fighetta *f.* a sexy girl, a hot chick • (lit.): a cute little vagina.

> *example:* Voltati! Svelto! Hai visto quella bella **fighetta** che è passata davanti alla fontana? Tutti si sono fermati per guardarla. Anche il traffico si è bloccato!

> *translation:* Turn around! Quick! Did you see that hot **chick** who walked by the fountain? Everybody stopped to look at her. Even the traffic stopped!

> **NOTE:** This comes from the feminine noun *fica* or *figa*, a vulgar term for "vagina," or more closely, "pussy."

levarsi di torno *exp.* to beat it • (lit.): to move from around.

> *example:* Quando Silvia è stata avvicinata da quel vecchio sporcaccione, gli ha detto di lasciarla in pace e di **levarsi di torno**.

> *translation:* When Silvia was approached by that dirty old man, she told him to leave her alone and **beat it**.

> **SYNONYM 1:** **alzare i tacchi** *exp.* • (lit.): to lift one's heels.

> **SYNONYM 2:** **filare** *v.* • (lit.): to spin.

> **SYNONYM 3:** **sgombrare** *v.* • (lit.): to evacuate, to move out of, to vacate.

> **SYNONYM 4:** **sloggiare** *v.* • (lit.): to dislodge, to shove off, to clear out.

> **SYNONYM 5:** **smammare** *v.* (Neapolitan, from the feminine noun *mammella*, meaning "breast").

mettersi insieme *exp.* to start a serious relationship, to tie the knot.

> *example:* Fabrizio e Serena escono insieme soltanto da due settimane e pensano di già di **mettersi insieme**.

> *translation:* Fabrizio and Serena have only been going out for the past two weeks, but they are already thinking of **tying the knot**.

> **SYNONYM:** **attaccarsi a qualcuno** *exp.* • (lit.): to stick to someone.

mollare qualcuno *v.* to dump someone • (lit.): to let go of someone, to release someone.

> *example:* Francesco ha **mollato** Monica la scorsa settimana, perchè lei da poco aveva cominciato a vedersi con un altro quando Francesco era fuori città per affari.
>
> *translation:* Francesco **dumped** Monica last week because she had just recently started seeing someone else when Francesco was out of town on business.
>
> **SYNONYM:** **scaricare qualcuno** *exp.* to unload someone.

pornazzo *m.* (from the masculine noun *porno*, meaning "pornographic movie") an X-rated movie.

> *example:* Hai visto? Quei due ragazzi si sono appena infilati là dentro, per vedersi un **pornazzo**!
>
> *translation:* Did you see that? Those two kids just snuck into that theater to see an **X-rated movie**!
>
> **SYNONYM:** **filmaccio** *m.* a bad or dirty movie.

scopata facile *f.* an easy lay (from the verb *scopare*, meaning "to sweep") • (lit.): an easy sweep.

> *example:* Soltanto perchè Tiziana è bella ed amichevole, i ragazzi presumono che sia una **scopata facile**.
>
> *translation:* Just because Tiziana is beautiful and friendly, guys just assume she's an **easy lay**.
>
> **NOTE:** The feminine noun *scopata* comes from the verb *scopare*, literally meaning "to sweep," yet is commonly used in Italian slang to mean "to have sex" and is considered very vulgar.

tirare un bidone a qualcuno *exp.* to stand someone up on a date or appointment • (lit.): to throw a trash can at someone.

> *example:* Marco sarebbe dovuto passare a prendermi alle 10:00 per andare al locale, ma non si è mai fatto vedere. Questa volta mi ha davvero **tirato un bidone**!
>
> *translation:* Marco was supposed to pick me up at 10:00 to go to the club, but he never showed up. He really **stood me up** this time!

| VARIATION 1: | **bidonare qualcuno** v. |

| VARIATION 2: | **fare un bidone a qualcuno** exp. • (lit.): to make a trash can. |

vecchio sporcaccione m. dirty old man.

example: Il nonno di Simona è davvero un **vecchio sporcaccione**. Tutte le volte che vede una ragazza sull'autobus, le si avvicina e le tocca il sedere!

translation: Simona's grandfather is really a **dirty old man**. Every time he sees a cute girl on the bus, he moves close to her and touches her butt!

| SYNONYM 1: | **vecchio maiale** m. • (lit.): old pig, swine, hog. |

| SYNONYM 2: | **vecchio porco** m. • (lit.): old pig, swine, hog. |

| SYNONYM 3: | **vecchio schifoso** m. • (lit.): disgusting old man. |

PRACTICE THE VOCABULARY

(Answers to Lesson One, p. 175)

A. Complete the phrases below by choosing the appropriate words from the list.

bellone	**donnaioli**	**pornazzo**
bidone	**fighetta**	**sporcaccioni**
galletto	**scopata**	**vista**
fisso	**metterti**	**torno**
cazzoni	**mollano**	

1. Non riesco a crederci! Massimo, il _____ che ho conosciuto la scorsa settimana, mi **ha tirato un** _____!

2. Non faccio che conoscere dei gran _____!

3. Eh, gli uomini! A tutti piace **fare il** _____.

4. Credo che siano tutti dei _____ e che tutti **abbiano quel chiodo** _____ **in testa**.

5. Ogni volta che vedono una bella _____, cercano di **beccarla**, e danno per scontato che sia una _____ **facile**.

6. Non appena però pensano che tu voglia _____ seriamente con loro, loro ti _____!

7. Ed io poi sono così stanca di incontrare **vecchi** _____ che pensano che sia **amore a prima** _____ dopo cinque minuti!

8. Mi è proprio successo la scorsa settimana! Ma penso che quello volesse soltanto far sesso; per cui gli ho detto di **levarsi di** _____ e di andare invece a vedersi un bel _____!

B. Match the English phrase in the left column with the Italian translation from the right. Write the appropriate letter in the box.

☐ 1. Giorgio thinks about Elena day and night. He's truly **fixated on her**.

☐ 2. Lorenzo and Cecilia met recently at a carnival party. They talked for a few minutes and exchanged phone numbers. It was **love at first sight**!

☐ 3. Simona's grandfather is really a **dirty old man**. Every time he sees a cute girl on the bus, he gets closer to her and touches her butt!

☐ 4. Enrico does nothing but look at girls! What a **playboy**! Last night at the club, he bought drinks for all the girls he met!

☐ 5. The guy I met at Giovanni's dinner party was a real **jerk**! He tried to hug and kiss all the cute girls who were there.

☐ 6. Francesco **dumped** Monica last week because she had just recently started seeing someone else when Francesco was out of town on business.

A. Il nonno di Simona è davvero un **vecchio sporcaccione**. Tutte le volte che vede una ragazza sull'autobus, le si avvicina e le tocca il sedere!

B. Francesco ha **mollato** Monica la scorsa settimana, perchè lei da poco aveva cominciato a vedersi con un altro quando Francesco era fuori città per affari.

C. Lorenzo e Cecilia si sono incontrati recentemente ad una festa di Carnevale. Si sono parlati per alcuni minuti e si sono scambiati i loro numeri di telefono. È stato **amore a prima vista**!

D. Il tipo che ho conosciuto alla cena di Giovanni era un gran **cazzone**! Ha cercato di abbracciare e baciare tutte le ragazze carine che erano lì.

E. Giorgio pensa ad Elena giorno e notte. Lui ha davvero un **chiodo fisso in testa**.

F. Enrico non fa altro che guardare le ragazze! Che **donnaiolo**! Ieri sera, al locale, ha offerto da bere a tutte le ragazze che ha conosciuto!

C. Underline the correct definition.

1. **amore a prima vista:**
   a. loves that ends in divorce
   b. love at first sight

2. **avere un chiodo fisso in testa:**
   a. to be fixated on someone/something
   b. to despise someone/something

3. **beccare qualcuno:**
   a. to dump someone
   b. to hit on someone

4. **bellone:**
   a. a very handsome man
   b. a very ugly man

5. **donnaiolo:**
   a. a beautiful woman
   b. a womanizer

6. **fare il galletto:**
   a. to flirt
   b. to get married

7. **fighetta:**
   a. an attractive young girl
   b. an ugly young girl

8. **levarsi di torno:**
   a. to arrive in the nick of time
   b. to leave, to "beat it"

9. **mettersi insieme:**
   a. to start a serious relationship
   b. to end a serious relationship

E. DICTATION
Test Your Listening Comprehension

(This dictation can be found in the Appendix on page 185.)

If you are following along with your cassette, you will now hear a series of sentences from the opening dialogue. These sentences will be read by a native speaker at normal conversational speed (which may seem fast to you at first). In addition, the words will be pronounced as you would actually hear them in a conversation, often including some common reductions.

The first time the sentences are presented, simply listen in order to get accustomed to the speed and heavy use of reductions. The sentences will then be read again with a pause after each to give you time to write down what you heard. The third time the sentences are read, follow along with what you have written.

Tipi come lui
mi rompono le scatole!

*(trans.): Guys like him **tick me off**!*
*(lit.): Guys like him **break my boxes**!*

Emanuela: Ehi! C'è il nuovo impiegato, Roberto. Che **tappo**! Ho notato che ti viene dietro da tutte le parti. Siete diventati amiconi, o che?

Filippo: **Chiudi il becco**! Non lo sopporto! È un **leccapiedi** da non crederci. Tipi come lui **mi rompono le scatole**. E **non gliene frega**, niente del suo lavoro. Passa gran parte del giorno a **spettegolare** al telefono con i suoi amici. Quel tipo è un **pigrone**!

Emanuela: Ci credi? Mi ha persino chiesto di uscire con lui! Non uscirei mai con un tipo **noioso** come quello. Ma non è tutto. È un' orribile **testona pelata**, con l'**alito puzzolente**! È anche un **allocco**, **tirato da morire** e vuole **fare sempre il grande. Mi fa impazzire**! Sinceramente credo anche che sia un po'**fuori di testa**.

Guys like him tick me off!

Emanuela: Hey! There's the new employee, Roberto. What a **runt**! I noticed he follows you around everywhere. Are you best friends now or or what?

Filippo: **Shut your trap**! I can't stand him! He's such an unbelievable **brownnoser**. Guys like that **tick me off**. And he **doesn't give a damn** about his work. He spends most of the day **gossiping** on the telephone with his friends. The guy's a **lazy bum**!

Emanuela: Can you believe this? He actually asked me to go out with him! I'd never go out with a **boring guy** like that. But that's not all. He's an ugly **little bald guy** with **bad breath**! He's also a **jerk**, **stingy big-time**, and a **showoff**. **He drives me crazy**! Frankly, I think he may a little **off his rocker**.

Guys like him break my boxes!

Emanuela: Hey! There's the new employee, Roberto. He's such a **cork**! I noticed that he follows you around everywhere. Are you best friends now or or what?

Filippo: **Shut the beak**! I can't stand him! He's such an unbelievable **feet-licker**. Guys like that **break my boxes**. And he **doesn't give a damn** about his work. He spends most of the day **tattling** on the telephone with his friends. The guy is a **lazy bum**!

Emanuela: Can you believe this? He actually asked me to go out with him! I'd never go out with a **boring guy** like that. But that's not all. He's an ugly **big peeled head** with **smelly breath**! He's also an **owl**, **pulled big-time**, and **does the big**. **He makes me crazy**! Frankly, I think he may a little **out of his head**.

VOCABULARY

alito puzzolente m. bad breath • (lit.): stinking breath.

    example: Matteo ha un **alito** così **puzzolente** che lo sento anche al telefono! Davvero non invidio la sua ragazza!

    translation: Matteo's got such a **bad breath** that I can even smell it over the phone! I really don't envy his girlfriend!

    SYNONYM: **alito fetente** m. • (lit.): stinking breath.

allocco m. a stupid person, a jerk • (lit.): owl.

    example: Cosimo è davvero un **allocco**! Lo hanno preso in giro tutta la sera e lui ha creduto a tutto quello che gli hanno raccontato!

    translation: Cosimo is such a **dolt**! They have been teasing him all night and he believed everything he was told!

    SYNONYM 1: **bischero** m. (Tuscany).

    SYNONYM 2: **coglione** m. • (lit.): testicle.

    SYNONYM 3: **credulone** m.

    SYNONYM 4: **cretino** m. • (lit.): cretin.

    SYNONYM 5: **fava** m. • (lit.): fava bean.

    SYNONYM 6: **fesso** m. • (lit.): from the feminine noun *fessura* meaning "crack" as in "a crack in one's head."

    SYNONYM 7: **imbecille** m. • (lit.): imbecile.

    SYNONYM 8: **oca** f. • (lit.): goose, referring to a female "dolt."

    SYNONYM 9: **scemo/a** n. • (from the verb *scemare*, meaning "to shrink or diminish").

chiudere il becco *exp.* to shut up, to shut one's trap • (lit.): to close the beak.

> *example:* Quando quella grassona ha cominciato ad offenderlo in pubblico, Luigi le ha detto di **chiudere il becco** e di levarsi di torno.
>
> *translation:* When that fat lady started to offend him in public, Luigi told her to **shut her trap** and get out of his way.
>
> **SYNONYM 1:** **chetarsi** *v.* • (lit.): to silence oneself.
>
> **SYNONYM 2:** **stare zitto/a** *exp.* • (lit.): to stay silent.

fare il grande *exp.* to show off, to act like someone big • (lit.): to do the big.

> *example:* Tutte le estati, al mare, Raffaele **fa il grande** con tutte le ragazze nuove. Prima le porta in giro con la sua nuova macchina, poi offre a tutte bibite e gelati!
>
> *translation:* Every summer at the beach, Raffaele **shows off** with all the new girls. First of all, he takes them for a ride in his new car, then buys drinks and ice cream for everybody!

fare impazzire qualcuno *exp.* to drive someone crazy • (lit.): to make someone crazy.

> *example:* Massimiliano a volte è che così insistente che **mi fa impazzire**. Gli ho già detto un milione di volte che non mi interessa uscire con lui!
>
> *translation:* Sometimes Massimiliano is so persistent that **he drives me crazy**. I have already told him a million times that I'm not interested in going out with him.
>
> **SYNONYM:** **mandare qualcuno fuori di cervello** *exp.* • (lit.): to send someone out of his/her brain.

fregarsene *v.* not to give a damn, not to give a shit.

> *example:* Stefano crede di poter uscire con tutte le ragazze che vuole soltanto perchè guida una Ferrari nuova di zecca. Ma io **me ne frego** della sua macchina. Preferirei uscire con Carlo, che è molto più intelligente di Stefano e anche molto più carino.

translation: Stefano thinks that he can go out with all the girls he wants only because he drives a brand new Ferrari. But I **don't give a damn** about his car. I would rather go out with Carlo, who is much more intelligent than Stefano and also much cuter.

> **SYNONYM:** **fottersene** *v.* (very vulgar).

fuori di testa (essere) *exp.* to be out of one's mind • (lit.): to be out of one's head.

example: Alessandro è uno dei più poveri fra i miei amici, ma continua a dire a tutti di essere una delle persone più ricche di Milano! Sinceramente credo che lui sia un po'**fuori di testa**.

translation: Alessandro is one of the poorest friends I have, but he keeps telling everybody that he is one of the richest persons in Milan! Frankly I think that he is a little bit **out of his mind**.

> **SYNONYM 1:** **non esserci con la testa** *exp.* • (lit.): not to be there with the head.

> **SYNONYM 2:** **partito/a (essere)** *adj.* • (lit.): to be gone.

leccapiedi *m.* brownnoser • (lit.): feet-licker.

example: Sai come ha preso quel lavoro Gabriele? Soltanto perchè è un gran **leccapiedi** e perchè va fuori con la figlia del capo!

translation: Do you know how Gabriele got that job? It's only because he is a big **brownnoser** and because he's dating the boss's daughter!

> **SYNONYM 1:** **leccaculo** *m.* (vulgar) • (lit.): ass-licker.

> **SYNONYM 2:** **lecchino/a** *n.* • (lit.): "a small licker."

noioso *adj.* boring.

example: Mamma mia! Questa festa è così **noiosa**! Il cibo fa schifo, le ragazze sono bruttissime e la musica è insopportabile! Andiamoce!

translation: Man! This party is so **boring**! The food is disgusting, the girls are ugly, and the music is just unbearable! Let's get out of here!

SYNONYM 1:   **palla** *f.* • (lit.): ball.

> **NOTE:** It's interesting to note that *palla* is used in the opposite way from English. In English, the expression *to have a ball* means "to have a great time." Whereas in Italian, it is used to indicate something boring.

SYNONYM 2:   **palloso/a** *adj.*

SYNONYM 3:   **pesante** *adj.* • (lit.): heavy.

SYNONYM 4:   **uggioso/a** *n.* (Tuscany) • (lit.): an annoying person.

---

pigrone/a *n. & adj.* a lazy bum (from the masculine noun *pigro*, meaning "someone who is idle") • (lit.): big lazy bum.

> *example:* Mario non finisce mai i suoi lavori. Tutte le volte che può, chiede a qualcun altro di finire per lui quello che stava facendo. Che **pigrone**!
>
> *translation:* Mario never finishes his jobs. Whenever he can, he asks someone else to finish whatever he was doing. What a **lazy bum**!

SYNONYM 1:   **addormentato/a** *n.* (from the verb *dormire*, meaning "to sleep") • (lit.): one who sleeps (or "sleeps on the job").

SYNONYM 2:   **poltrone** *m.* • (lit.): someone who is very sluggish.

SYNONYM 3:   **sfaticato/a** *n.*

---

rompere le scatole a qualcuno *exp.* to annoy someone, to tick someone off • (lit.): to break the boxes.

> *example:* Tutte le volte che incontro Giorgio ad una festa, lui ci prova con me, ma dopo un po', generalmente, comincia a **rompermi le scatole**.
>
> *translation:* Everytime I run into Giorgio at a party, he tries to flirt with me, but after a while he usually starts **ticking me off**.

SYNONYM 1:   **rompere/scassare i coglioni** *exp.* (vulgar) • (lit.): to break the balls.

SYNONYM 2:   **rompere/scassare i marroni** *exp.* • (lit.): to break the chestnuts.

SYNONYM 3: **rompere/scassare le palle/balle** *exp.* • (lit.): to break the balls.

spettegolare *v.* to gossip • (lit.): to tattle.

example: Serena non fa altro che **spettegolare**. Tutti nel rione, per colpa sua, pensano che mia sorella esca con tre ragazzi diversi. Ma non è vero!

translation: Serena does nothing but **gossip**. Because of that, everyone in the neighborhood thinks my sister goes out with three different guys. But it's not true!

SYNONYM 1: **chiacchierare** *v.* • (lit.): to chatter, to blab, to gossip.

SYNONYM 2: **dire male** *exp.* • (lit.): to say bad.

SYNONYM 3: **mormorare** *v.* • (lit.): to babble, to grumble.

tappo *m.* a very short guy • (lit.): cork.

example: Due giorni fa, mentre bevevo un caffè al bar, un brutto **tappo** ha versato tutto il suo cappuccino sulla mia gonna!

translation: Two days ago, while I was having a coffee at the bar, an ugly **runt** spilled all his cappuccino on my skirt!

VARIATION 1: **tappetto** *m.*

VARIATION 2: **tappino** *m.* • (lit.): small cork.

SYNONYM 1: **mezza cartuccia (una)** *f.* • (lit.): half a cartridge.

SYNONYM 2: **mezza sega (una)** *f.* • (lit.): half a saw.

testona pelata *f.* a bald guy, a "baldy" • (lit.): big peeled head.

example: Non riesco a credere che Cinzia sia fidanzata con quell' orribile **crapa pelata**! Lui non ha un briciolo di classe e la tratta come se fosse la sua donna di servizio.

translation: I cannot believe that Cinzia is engaged to that ugly **bald guy**! He doesn't have an iota of class at all and treats her as if she were his servant.

SYNONYM: **zucca pelata** *f.* • (lit.): peeled pumpkin.

tirato/a *adj.* stingy • (lit): pulled.

>   *example:*   Giordano è sempre molto **tirato**. Anche quando esce
>   con la sua ragazza, non paga mai il conto al ristorante.
>
>   *translation:*   Giordano is always very **stingy**. Even when he goes
>   out with his girlfriend, he never pays the bill at the
>   restaurant.
>
>   **NOTE:**   You'll notice in the opening that *tirato da morire* was
>   used. *Da morire* is a common Italian expression,
>   meaning "extremely" or "big-time."
>
>   **SYNONYM 1:**   **spilorcio/a** *adj.*
>
>   **SYNONYM 2:**   **taccagno/a** *adj.*
>
>   **SYNONYM 3:**   **tirchio/a** *adj.*

PRACTICE THE VOCABULARY

(Answers to Lesson Two, p. 175)

A. Match the English phrase in the left column with the Italian translation from the right. Write the appropriate letter in the box.

☐ 1. Giordano is always very **stingy**. Even when he goes out with his girlfriend, he never pays the bill at the restaurant.

☐ 2. Matteo's got such a **bad breath** that I can even smell it over the phone! I really don't envy his girlfriend!

☐ 3. Serena does nothing but **gossip**. Because of that, everyone in the neighborhood thinks that my sister goes out with three different guys. But it isn't true!

☐ 4. Man! This party is so **boring**! The food is disgusting, the girls are ugly, and the music is just unbearable! Let's get out of here!

☐ 5. Every summer at the beach, Raffaele **shows off** with all the new girls. First of all, he takes them for a ride in his new car, then buys drinks and ice cream for everybody!

A. Tutte le estati, al mare, Raffaele **fa il grande** con tutte le ragazze nuove. Prima le porta in giro con la sua nuova macchina, poi offre a tutte bibite e gelati!

B. Matteo ha un **alito** così **puzzolente** che lo sento anche al telefono! Davvero non invidio la sua ragazza!

C. Giordano è sempre molto **tirato**. Anche quando esce con la sua ragazza, non paga mai il conto al ristorante.

D. Serena non fa altro che **spettegolare**. Tutti nel rione, per colpa sua, pensano che mia sorella esca con tre ragazzi diversi! Ma non è vero!

E. Mamma mia! Questa festa è così **noiosa**! Il cibo fa schifo, le ragazze sono bruttissime e la musica è insopportabile! Andiamocene!

B. Complete the following phrases by choosing the appropriate words from the list below. Make all necessary changes.

becco   **pelata**

frega   **pigrone**

grande   **puzzolente**

leccapiedi   **scatole**

morire   **spettegolare**

noioso   **tappo**

1. Ehi! C'è il nuovo impiegato, Roberto. È così _____! Ho notato che ti viene dietro da tutte le parti. Siete diventati amiconi, o che?

2. Chiudi il _____! Non lo sopporto!

3. È un _____ da non crederci. Tipi come lui mi rompono le _____!

4. E non gliene _____ niente del suo lavoro.

5. Passa gran parte del giorno a _____ al telefono con i suoi amici. Quel tipo è un _____!

6. Ci credi? Mi ha persino chiesto di uscire con lui! Non uscirei mai con un tipo _____ come lui.

7. Ma non è tutto. È un'orribile testona _____, con un alito _____!

8. È anche un allocco, tirchio da _____ e vuole fare sempre il _____.

C. Underline the correct definition.

1. **allocco:**
   a. intelligent person
   b. stupid person

2. **tirato/a:**
   a. pretty
   b. stingy

3. **alito puzzolente:**
   a. bad breath
   b. pleasant breath

4. **fregarsene:**
   a. not to give a damn
   b. to care greatly

5. **chiudere il becco:**
   a. to close one's mind to new ideas
   b. to shut one's mouth or "trap"

6. **fare il grande:**
   a. to show off
   b. to act like a big boy

7. **fare impazzire qualcuno:**
   a. to make someone fall in love
   b. to drive someone crazy

8. **essere fuori di testa:**
   a. to be extremely happy
   b. to be out of one's mind

9. **leccapiedi:**
   a. brownnoser
   b. shoe salesperson

10. **noioso:**
    a. noisy
    b. boring

11. **pigrone/a:**
    a. a lazy bum
    b. a very short person

12. **rompere le scatole:**
    a. to get married
    b. to annoy

13. **spettegolare:**
    a. to spit while talking
    b. to gossip

14. **tappo:**
    a. very short guy
    b. very tall guy

15. **testona pelata:**
    a. a guy with lots of hair
    b. a bald guy, a "baldy"

D. DICTATION
Test Your Listening Comprehension

(This dictation can be found in the Appendix on page 185.)

If you are following along with your cassette, you will now hear a series of sentences from the opening dialogue. These sentences will be read by a native speaker at normal conversational speed (which may seem fast to you at first). In addition, the words will be pronounced as you would actually hear them in a conversation, often including some common reductions.

The first time the sentences are presented, simply listen in order to get accustomed to the speed and heavy use of reductions. The sentences will then be read again with a pause after each to give you time to write down what you heard. The third time the sentences are read, follow along with what you have written.

Accidenti alla quella gran porca di tua madre!

(trans.): Screw you!
(lit.): Damn that big sow of your mother!

Giuseppe: Guarda quella **bagascia**!

Carmela: **Che diavolo stai facendo**? Che **coglione**! Non sai guidare?

Alfredo: **Maledetta puttana**! Scommetto che **ha le sue cose**.

Carmela: **Bastardo**! Non sopporto i **leccacazzi** come te! **Va'a farti fottere**!

Giuseppe: **Cacciatelo in culo**!

Alfredo: **Accidenti alla quella gran porca di tua madre**!

Giuseppe: Per poco non mi distrugge la macchina, e **mi mostra il dito**?! **Va'al diavolo!**

Carmela: **Figlio di troia**!

Giuseppe: **Leccaculi**!

Alfredo: Giuseppe, lasciala perdere! Dobbiamo correre per non arrivare tardi in chiesa.

Screw you!

Giuseppe: Look at that **bitch**!

Carmela: **What the hell are you doing**? What an **asshole**! Don't you know how to drive?

Alfredo: What a **fucking whore**! I bet she's **on the rag**.

Carmela: **Bastard**! I can't stand **cocksuckers** like you! **Fuck you**!

Giuseppe: **Shove it up your ass**!

Alfredo: **Screw you**!

Giuseppe: She almost destroys my car and **gives me the finger**?! **Go to hell**!

Carmela: **Son of a whore**!

Giuseppe: **Ass-licker**!

Alfredo: Giuseppe, forget about her. We need to run or we're going to be late for church.

Damn that big sow of your mother!

Giuseppe: Look at that **whore**!

Carmela: **What the devil are you doing**? What a **testicle**! Don't you know how to drive?

Alfredo: What a **damned whore**! I bet she **has her things**.

Carmela: **Bastard**! I can't stand **cock-lickers** like you! **Go get yourself fucked**!

Giuseppe: **Stuff it in the ass**!

Alfredo: **Damn that big sow of your mother**!

Giuseppe: She almost destroys my car and **shows me the finger**?! **Go to the devil**!

Carmela: **Son of a whore**!

Giuseppe: **Ass-licker**!

Alfredo: Giuseppe, forget about her. We need to run so that we're not late for church.

VOCABULARY

"Accidenti a quella gran porca di tua madre!" *interj.*
"Screw you!" • (lit.): "Damn that big sow of your mother!"

> *example:* Oh, stupido bastardo! Ma devi imparare a guidare! **Accidenti a quella gran porca di tua madre**!
>
> *translation:* Oh, you stupid bastard! You need to learn how to drive! **Screw you**!

> **SYNONYM 1:** **"Accidenti a quella gran maiala di tua madre!"** *interj.* • (lit.): "Damn that big sow of your mother!"

> **SYNONYM 2:** **"Accidenti a quella gran puttana di tua madre!"** *interj.* • (lit.): "Damn that big whore of your mother!"

> **SYNONYM 3:** **"Accidenti a quella gran troia di tua madre!"** *interj.* • (lit.): "Damn that big sow of your mother!"

avere le proprie cose *exp.* to be on the rag, to menstruate • (lit.): to have one own things.

> *example:* Mamma mia! È impossibile parlare con Giulia oggi! Deve **avere le sue cose**!
>
> *translation:* Geez! It's impossible to talk to Giulia today! She must **be on the rag**!

> **SYNONYM 1:** **avere il marchese** *exp.* (more vulgar) • (lit.): to have the marquise.

> **SYNONYM 2:** **avere le mestruazioni** *exp.* • (lit.): to menstruate.

bagascia *f.* whore, slut.

      example: Marina è davvero una gran **bagascia**. Alle feste si fa toccare da tutti i ragazzi!

      translation: Marina is really a **slut**. She lets all the guys touch her at the parties!

    SYNONYM 1:   **cagna** *f.* female dog, bitch.

    SYNONYM 2:   **maiala** *f.* • (lit.): sow, female pig.

    SYNONYM 3:   **puttana** f. • (lit.): prostitute.

    SYNONYM 4:   **vacca** *f.* • (lit.): cow.

    ALSO: **figlio/a di troia** *m.* son/daughter of a bitch • (lit.): son/daughter of a sow.

bastardo/a *n.* • (lit.): bastard.

      example: Enrico è un **bastardo** fetente! Ieri ha telefonato alla mia ragazza e le ha chiesto di uscire!

      translation: Enrico is a stinking **bastard**! Yesterday he called my girlfriend and asked her out!

    SYNONYM 1:   **figlio di puttana** *m.* • (lit.): son of a whore.

    SYNONYM 2:   **stronzo/a** *n.* • (lit.): turd.

"Cacciatelo in culo!" *interj.* "Up yours!" • (lit): "Stick it in your ass!"

      example: Figlio di puttana, **cacciatelo in culo**!

      translation: You son of a bitch, **stick it up your ass**!

Che diavolo stai facendo? *exp.* What the hell are you doing? • (lit.): What the devil are you doing?

      example: Mario, **che diavolo stai facendo**? Lasciala stare. Non vedi che Monica è venuta alla festa con il suo ragazzo?

      translation: Mario, **what the hell are you doing**? Leave her alone. Don't you see that Monica has come to the party with her boyfriend?

    SYNONYM: **Che cazzo stai facendo?** *exp.* (more vulgar) What the fuck are you doing? • (lit.): What dick are you doing?

coglione m. asshole, jerk, idiot • (lit.): testicle.

> *example:* Giovanni è così **coglione**. Mi ha rotto lui la bici, e ha dato la colpa a qualcun altro.
>
> *translation:* Giovanni is such a **jerk**. He broke my bike and blamed it on someone else.

SYNONYM 1: **cazzone** m. • (lit.): big dick.

SYNONYM 2: **fava** f. • (lit.): fava bean, but also the head of the dick in Tuscan slang.

SYNONYM 3: **fesso** m. • (lit.): from the feminine noun *fessura* meaning "crack" as in "a crack in one's head."

SYNONYM 4: **imbecille** m. • (lit.): imbecile.

SYNONYM 5: **scemo/a** n. • (from the verb *scemare*, meaning "to shrink" or "to diminish").

figlio di troia m. son of a bitch • (lit.): son of a sow.

> *example:* Armando è un **figlio di troia**! Se lo vedo gli rompo la testa!
>
> *translation:* Armando is a **son of a bitch**! If I see him, I'm going to punch his lights out!

SYNONYM 1: **figlio di maiala** m. • (lit.): son of a sow.

SYNONYM 2: **figlio di puttana** m. • (lit.): son of a whore.

SYNONYM 3: **figlio di zoccola** m. • (lit.): son of a sewer rat.

leccacazzi m. cocksucker • (lit.): dick-licker.

> *example:* Il mio vicino è il più gran **leccacazzi** del mondo. Ha preso le sue chiavi ed ha scritto il suo nome sulla fiancata della mia macchina!
>
> *translation:* My neighbor is the biggest **cocksucker**. He took his keys and wrote his name on the side of my car!

SYNONYM 1: **leccafave** m. • (lit.): "dicks-licker" from the feminine *fava*, meaning "fava bean" but used in Italian slang to mean "penis."

SYNONYM 2: **leccauccelli** m. • (lit.): birds-licker (*lecca* = lick • *l'uccello* = bird).

NOTE: **uccello** m. dick • (lit.): bird.

leccaculo *m.* • **1.** asshole, jerk • **2.** ass-kisser, brownnoser • (lit.): ass-licker.

> *example 1:* Voi due, luridi merdosi **leccaculi**! Andate via di qui o chiamo subito la polizia!
>
> *translation:* You dirty **assholes**! Get out of here or I'll call the police!
>
> *example 2:* Oreste è un gran **leccaculo**! Tutte le volte che fa un viaggio all'estero, porta un regalino al professore di matematica.
>
> *translation:* Oreste is a big **ass-kisser**! Every time he travels abroad, he brings back a little present for his math professor.

maledetta puttana *f.* damned bitch, fucking bitch • (lit.): damned prostitute.

> *example:* **Maledetta puttana**! Con chi hai dormito ieri sera?
>
> *translation:* You **fucking bitch**! Who did you sleep with last night?
>
> **SYNONYM 1:** **maledetta troia** *f.* • (lit.): damned sow.
>
> **SYNONYM 2:** **maledetta vacca** *f.* • (lit.): damned cow.

mostrare il dito medio *exp.* to give the finger • (lit.): to show the middle finger.

> *example:* Ieri, mentre guidavo, qualcuno dall'autobus **mi ha mostrato il dito medio**!
>
> *translation:* Yesterday, while I was driving, someone in a bus **gave me the finger**!
>
> **NOTE:** This expression is gaining popularity in Italy because it is seen in American movies. However, the most common abusive gesture is the "cuckold gesture," especially referring to men whose wives are unfaithful. This gesture is accomplished by raising the index and little finger symbolizing antlers. This gesture is called *fare le corna,* meaning "to do (show) the antlers."
>
> **SEE:** Gestures, *p. 154.*

"Va'a farti fottere!" *interj.* "Fuck you!" • (lit.): "Go get yourself fucked!"

      example: **Va'a farti fottere**! Brutto bastardo! Rendimi la borsa!

      translation: **Fuck off**! Ugly bastard! Give my purse back to me!

      SYNONYM 1: **"Va'a cagare!"** *interj.* • (lit.): "Go shit!"

      SYNONYM 2: **"Va'a prendertelo in culo!"** *interj.* • (lit.): "Go get it in your ass!"

      SYNONYM 3: **"Vaffantasca!"** *interj.* (Tuscan) • (lit.): "Go do in the pocket!"

"Va'al diavolo!" *interj.* "Go to hell!" • (lit.): "Go to the Devil!"

      example: **Va'al diavolo**, vecchio maiale! Lasciami stare!

      translation: **Go to hell**, you dirty old man! Leave me alone!

      SYNONYM: **"Va'alla/in malora!"** *interj.* • (lit.): "Go to the/in devil!"

PRACTICE THE VOCABULARY

(Answers to Lesson Three, p. 176)

A. Match the English phrase in the left column with the Italian translation from the right. Write the appropriate letter in the box.

☐ 1. Giovanni is such a **jerk**. He broke my bike and blamed it on someone else.

☐ 2. Man! It's impossible to talk to Giulia today! She must **be on the rag**!

☐ 3. Yesterday, while I was driving, someone in a bus **gave me the finger**!

☐ 4. You stupid bastard! You need to learn how to drive! **Screw you!**

☐ 5. Mario, **what the hell are you doing**? Leave her alone! Don't you see that Monica has come to the party with her boyfriend?

☐ 6. You dirty **assholes**! Get out of here or I'll call the police!

A. Oh, stupido bastardo! Ma impara a guidare! **Accidenti a quella gran porca di tua madre**!

B. Mamma mia! È impossibile parlare con Giulia oggi! Deve **avere le sue cose**!

C. Mario, **che diavolo stai facendo**? Lasciala stare! Non vedi che Monica è venuta alla festa con il suo ragazzo?

D. Giovanni è così **coglione**. Mi ha rotto lui la bici, e ha dato la colpa a qualcun altro.

E. Ieri, mentre guidavo, qualcuno dall'autobus **mi ha mostrato il dito medio**!

F. Voi due, luridi merdosi **leccaculi**! Andate via di qui o chiamo subito la polizia!

B. Complete the opening dialogue by choosing the appropriate words from the list below. The English equivalents are in parentheses.

bagascia	diavolo	leccacazzi
bastardo	figlio di troia	leccaculi
coglione	fottere	porca
culo	ha le sue cose	puttana

Giuseppe: Guarda quella *(whore)*_____!

Carmela: Che *(the hell)*_____ stai facendo? Che *(an asshole

or "testicle")*_____! Non sai guidare?

Alfredo: Maledetta *(prostitute)*_____ ! Scommetto che

*(she's on the rag)*_____!

Carmela: *(Bastard)*_____! Non sopporto i

*(cocksuckers)*_____ come te! Va'a farti

*(fucked)*_____!

Giuseppe: Cacciatelo in *(ass)*_____!

Alfredo: Accidenti alla quella gran *(sow)*_____ di tua madre!

Giuseppe: Per poco non mi distrugge la macchina, e mi mostra il dito?!

Va'al diavolo!

Carmela: *(Son of a bitch)*_____!

Giuseppe: *(Ass-licker)*_____!

Alfredo: Giuseppe, lasciala perdere! Dobbiamo correre per non arrivare

tardi in chiesa.

C. Underline the correct definition.

1. **bagascia:**
   a. whore
   b. prostitute's client

2. **leccaculo:**
   a. brownnoser
   b. to have a large behind

3. **Va'a farti fottere!:**
   a. How nice to see you again!
   b. Fuck you!

4. **mostrare il dito medio:**
   a. to give the finger
   b. to thumb a ride

5. **Va'al diavolo!:**
   a. Hurry to the party!
   b. Go to hell!

6. **figlio di troia:**
   a. a good son
   b. son of a bitch

7. **Accidenti a quella gran porca di tua madre!**
   a. I heard your mother was in an accident!
   b. Screw you!

8. **Cacciatelo in culo!:**
   a. Shove it up your ass!
   b. Sit your butt down right here!

9. **avere le proprie cose:**
   a. to be on the rag
   b. to be bored

10. **maledetta puttana:**
    a. damned weather
    b. damned bitch

11. **leccacazzi:**
    a. cocksucker
    b. butt-licker

12. **coglione:**
    a. asshole
    b. fatso

13. **bastardo/a:**
    a. a helpful person
    b. a bastard

14. **Che diavolo stai facendo?:**
    a. How the hell are you?
    b. What the hell are you doing?

E. DICTATION
Test Your Listening Comprehension

(This dictation can be found in the Appendix on page 186.)

If you are following along with your cassette, you will now hear a series of sentences from the opening dialogue. These sentences will be read by a native speaker at normal conversational speed (which may seem fast to you at first). In addition, the words will be pronounced as you would actually hear them in a conversation, often including some common reductions.

The first time the sentences are presented, simply listen in order to get accustomed to the speed and heavy use of reductions. The sentences will then be read again with a pause after each to give you time to write down what you heard. The third time the sentences are read, follow along with what you have written.

Che *rompiscatole* è lei!

(trans.): What a **pain in the butt** she is!
(lit.): What a **box-breaker** she is!

Rossella: Ornella! Grazie mille per averci invitati! Ci stiamo divertendo un sacco! *(Poi, sottovoce...)* Mamma mia! **Muoio dalla noia** qui!

Pietro: Il marito di Ornella è così **fesso**. È sempre un **guastafeste**.

Rossella: Certo, capisco cosa vuoi dire. Allora, hai assaggiato il cibo? È così **schifoso**! Pensavo addirittura di **vomitare l'anima**!

Pietro: E poi la loro casa è **un troiaio**! Nooo! Guarda chi è appena entrata. Teresa. Che **rompiscatole** è lei! E suo marito è quel **grassone** là.

Rossella: Lo vedo. Lui ha davvero messo su un bel po' di peso. Credo anche che sia **un po'di fuori**.

Pietro: È cambiato così tanto! L'ultima volta che l'ho visto non aveva la **zucca pelata** come ora. A dire il vero **porta davvero male gli anni**.

She's such a pain in the butt!

Rossella: Ornella! Thank you so much for inviting us! We're having such a wonderful time! *(Then in a low voice...)* Oh, brother! I'm **dying of boredom** here!

Pietro: And Ornella's husband is such a **jerk**. He's always such a **killjoy**.

Rossella: Yeah, I know what you mean. So tell me, did you taste the food? It's **gross**! I thought I was going to **barf my guts up**!

Pietro: And their house is a **pigsty**! Oh, no! Look who just walked in. Teresa. What a **pain in the butt** she is! And her husband is that **big fat slob** over there.

Rossella: I noticed. He's really put on quite a bit of weight. I also think he's a **little nuts**.

Pietro: He's changed so much! The last time I saw him, he wasn't such a **baldy** like he is now. To tell you the truth, he sure **isn't aging well**.

She's such a box-breaker!

Rossella: Ornella! Thank you so much for inviting us! We're having such a wonderful time! *(Then in a low voice...)* Oh, brother! I'm **dying of boredom** here!

Pietro: And Ornella's husband is such a **crack**. He's always been such a **party spoiler**.

Rossella: Yeah, I know what you mean. So tell me, did you taste the food? It's **gross**! I thought I was going to **throw up my soul**!

Pietro: And their house is a **pigsty**! Oh, no! Look who just walked in. Teresa. What a **box-breaker** she is! And her husband is that **big fat slob** over there.

Rossella: I noticed. He's really put on quite a bit of weight. I also think he's a **little out**.

Pietro: He's changed so much! The last time I saw him, he wasn't such a **peeled pumpkin** like he is now. To tell you the truth, he sure **is carrying the years badly**.

VOCABULARY

essere un po'di fuori *exp.* to a little wacky, to be out of one's mind •
(lit.): to be a little bit out.

> *example:* Quella vecchia donna è **un po'di fuori**. Continua a
> parlare con tutti quei turisti e non sa nemmeno cosa
> dice.

> *translation:* That old woman is **a little wacky**. She keeps talking
> to all those tourists and doesn't even know what she's
> saying.

> **SYNONYM 1:** **essere fuori di testa** *exp.* • (lit.): to be outside of
> head.

> **SYNONYM 2:** **non esserci con la testa** *exp.* • (lit.): not to be there
> with the head.

fesso/a *adj.* stupid, out of it.

> *example:* Credo che Antonello sia un po'**fesso**! È la quarta volta
> questa settimana che chiude la macchina con le chiavi
> dentro!

> *translation:* I think that Antonello is a little **out of it**! He locked his
> keys in his car for the fourth time this week!

> **VARIATION:** **fessacchiotto/a** *adj.*

> **SYNONYM 1:** **coglione/a** *n. & adj.*

> **SYNONYM 2:** **minchione/a** *n. & adj.* (Sicilian).

> **SYNONYM 3:** **tonto/a** *n. & adj.*

> **ALSO:** **fare fesso qualcuno** *exp.* to swindle someone •
> (lit.): to make someone stupid.

grassone/a *n.* a very fat man or woman, a fatso, fat slob.

> *example:* La mia vicina di casa è una **grassona** incredibile!
> Tutte le mattine la vedo agli alimentari vicino a casa
> nostra, a mangiarsi tre o quattro panini al salame!

translation: Our neighbor is really a **fat slob**! Every morning I see her at the deli near our house eating three or four salami sandwiches!

SYNONYM 1:   **balena** *f.* • (lit.): a whale.

SYNONYM 2:   **cicciobomba** *n.* • (lit.): fat bomb.

SYNONYM 3:   **ciccione/a** *n.* • (lit.): big fat person (from the feminine noun *ciccia*, meaning "flab").

guastafeste (un/una) *n.* a party pooper • (lit.): a party spoiler.

example: Ieri sera eravamo tutti pronti per andare a ballare in discoteca, quando Filippo ci ha detto che non voleva accompagnarci in macchina. Filippo è proprio un **guastafeste**!

translation: Yesterday evening we were all ready to go dancing, but Filippo told us that he didn't want to take us there in his car. Filippo is really a **party pooper**!

morire di/dalla noia *exp.* to die of boredom • (lit.): [same].

example: Questa festa è veramente brutta! **Sto morendo dalla noia**! Perchè non ce ne andiamo subito?

translation: This party is really bad! **I'm bored to death**! Why don't we get out of here right now?

portare male gli anni *exp.* not to age well • (lit.): to bring the years badly.

example: Francesca ha soltanto ventitré anni, ma ne dimostra quaranta! **Porta davvero male gli anni**!

translation: Francesca is only twenty-three but she looks forty! **She really doesn't age well**!

rompiscatole (un/una) *n.* a pain in the neck • (lit.): box-breaker.

example: Gianna è una gran **rompiscatole**. Tutti i giorni mi chiama dopo mezzanotte per parlarmi dei suoi problemi con Marco.

translation: Gianna is a big **pain in the neck**. Every day, she calls me after midnight to talk to me about her problems with Marco.

SYNONYM 1: **rompi palle/balle (un/una)** *n.* • (lit.): a ball-breaker.

SYNONYM 2: **rompicoglioni (un/una)** *n.* • (lit.): a ball-breaker.

SYNONYM 3: **scassacazzo (un/una)** *n.* (very vulgar) • (lit.): a dick-breaker.

schifoso/a *adj.* disgusting, gross.

   example: Queste lasagne sono **schifose**! Credo che le abbiano fatte con della carne marcia!

   translation: This lasagna is **disgusting**! I think they made it with rotten meat!

   SYNONYM: **da fare vomitare** *exp.* enough to make you throw up • (lit.): vomit-making.

   VARIATION: **da fare schifo** *exp.* to be disgusting, gross • *Questa pasta è salata da fare schifo;* This pasta is disgustingly salty!

troiaio *m.* a very dirty, filthy place • (lit): pigsty.

   example: Il nuovo appartamento di Federico è un **troiaio**! I muri sono sporchi e c'è un gran puzzo di uova marce!

   translation: Federico's new apartment looks like a **pigsty**! The walls are dirty and there's a terrible stench of rotten eggs!

   SYNONYM 1: **maialaio** *m.* • (lit.): pigsty.

   SYNONYM 2: **porcaio** *m.* • (lit.): pigsty.

vomitare l'anima *exp.* to throw up, to barf one's guts up • (lit.): to vomit one's soul.

   example: Tutte le volte che torno a casa dopo aver mangiato a casa di Luca, **vomito l'anima mia**!

   translation: Every time I come back home after having eaten at Luca's, **I barf my guts up**!

   SYNONYM: **fare i gattini** • (lit.): to make the kittens.

zucca pelata *f.* a bald person, baldy • (lit.): a peeled pumpkin.

> *example:* Di'a quella **zucca pelata** che non ha bisogno di andare dal barbiere!
>
> *translation:* Tell that **bald guy** he doesn't need a barber!
>
> **SYNONYM 1:** **rapato/a** *adj.* • (lit.): from the verb *rapare*, meaning "to crop" or "to shave."
>
> **SYNONYM 2:** **tosato/a** *adj.* • (lit.): from the verb *tosare*, meaning "to shear" or "to clip."

PRACTICE THE VOCABULARY

(Answers to Lesson Four, p. 177)

A. Match the English phrase in the left column with the Italian translation from the right. Write the appropriate letter in the box.

1. That old woman **isn't all there**. She keeps talking to all those tourists and she doesn't even know what she's saying.

2. Gianna is a big **pain in the neck**. Every day she calls me after midnight to talk to me about her problems with Marco.

3. Tell that **bald guy** he doesn't need a barber!

4. This lasagna is **disgusting**! I think thay made it with rotten meat!

5. Federico's new apartment looks like a **pigsty**! The walls are dirty and there's a terrible stench of rotten eggs!

6. Yesterday evening, we were all ready to go dancing, but Filippo told us that he didn't want to take us there in his car. Filippo is really a **party pooper**!

A. Queste lasagne sono **schifose**! Credo che le abbiano fatte con della carne marcia!

B. Quella vecchia donna è **un po' di fuori**. Continua a parlare con tutti quei turisti e non sa nemmeno cosa dice.

C. Ieri sera eravamo tutti pronti per andare a ballare in discoteca, quando Filippi ha detto che non voleva accompagnarci in macchina. Filippi è proprio un **guastafeste**!

D. Gianna è una gran **rompiscatole**. Tutti i giorni mi chiama dopo mezzanotte per parlarmi dei suoi problemi con Marco.

E. Il nuovo appartamento di Federico è un **troiaio**! I muri sono sporchi e c'è un gran puzzo di uova marce!

F. Di'a quella **zucca pelata** che non ha bisogno di andare dal barbiere!

B. Complete the following phrases by choosing the appropriate words from the list below.

anima	**fuori**	**rompiscatole**
anni	**muoio**	**schifoso**
fesso	**pelata**	**troiaio**

1. Ornella! Grazie mille per averci invitati! Ci stiamo divertendo un
    sacco! *(Poi, sottovoce...)* Mamma mia! _____ dalla noia
    qui!

2. Il marito di Ornella è così _____. È sempre un
    guastafeste.

3. Certo, capisco cosa vuoi dire! Allora, hai assaggiato il cibo? È così
    _____! Pensavo addirittura di vomitare
    l'_____!

4. E poi la loro casa è un _____! Nooo! Guarda
    chi è appena entrata! Teresa! Che _____ è lei!
    E suo marito è quel grassone là

5. Lo vedo. Lui ha davvero messo su un bel po' di peso. Credo anche
    che sia un po' di _____.

6. È cambiato così tanto! L'ultima volta che l'ho visto non aveva la
    zucca _____ come ora. A dire il vero porta
    davvero male gli _____!

C. Underline the correct definition.

1. **essere un po' di fuori:**
   a. to be stood up on a date
   b. to be wacky

2. **fesso/a:**
   a. stupid
   b. intelligent

3. **grassone/a:**
   a. greasy
   b. a fatso

4. **guastafeste:**
   a. the life of the party
   b. a party pooper

5. **portare male gli anni:**
   a. to age well
   b. not to age well

6. **rompiscatole:**
   a. a pain in the neck
   b. a very muscular man

7. **schifoso/a:**
   a. appetizing
   b. disgusting

8. **troiaio:**
   a. a very clean place
   b. a very dirty place

9. **vomitare l'anima:**
   a. to throw one's guts up
   b. to be on the mend

E. DICTATION
Test Your Listening Comprehension

(This dictation can be found in the Appendix on page 186.)

If you are following along with your cassette, you will now hear a series of sentences from the opening dialogue. These sentences will be read by a native speaker at normal conversational speed (which may seem fast to you at first). In addition, the words will be pronounced as you would actually hear them in a conversation, often including some common reductions.

The first time the sentences are presented, simply listen in order to get accustomed to the speed and heavy use of reductions. The sentences will then be read again with a pause after each to give you time to write down what you heard. The third time the sentences are read, follow along with what you have written.

Il quartiere a luci rosse.

(trans.): The **red-light district**.
(lit.): The **quarter with red lights**.

Corrado: È una bellissima giornata! Che ne dici di fare due passi in centro?

Silvia: In centro? Ma è là dove c'è il **quartiere a luci rosse**! È pieno di **puttane**, **magnaccia** e **bordelli**!

Corrado: Lo so, ma è interessante da vedere. Sai, l'ultima volta che sono passato da quelle parti, ho visto Fulvio con due **troie**. A dire il vero, ne stava **baciando una con la lingua**.

Silvia: Be', se gli piacciono, spero che almeno usi un **guanto**. Sono certa che non vuole beccarsi **l'AIDS**.

Corrado: Immagino che voglia soltanto farsi fare un **pompino**, o magari fare una **bella scopata**. Soltanto l'idea di andare in un **casino** mi renderebbe così nervoso che non mi riuscirebbe nemmeno **farlo rizzare**!

The *Red-light* District

Corrado: It's such a beautiful day! What do you say we take a stroll downtown?

Silvia: Downtown? That's where the **red-light district** is! It's full of **whores**, **pimps** and **brothels**!

Corrado: I know it, but it's interesting to see. You know, the last time I passed by there, I saw Fulvio with two **sluts**. In fact, he was actually **giving a French kiss** to one of them.

Silvia: Well, if he likes them, at least I hope he uses a **rubber**. He certainly doesn't want to get **AIDS**.

Corrado: I suppose he just wanted to get a quick **blow job** or maybe a **good lay**. Just the idea of going to a **whorehouse** would make me so nervous, I wouldn't be able to **get it up**!

The quarter of red lights

Corrado: It's such a beautiful day! What do you say we take a stroll downtown?

Silvia: Downtown? That's where the **quarter of red lights** is! It's full of **whores**, **money-eaters** and **brothels**!

Corrado: I know it, but it's interesting to see. You know, the last time I passed by there, I saw Fulvio with two **sows**. In fact, he was actually **giving a kiss with the tongue** to one of them.

Silvia: Well, if he does, at least I hope he uses a **glove**. He certainly doesn't want to get **AIDS**.

Corrado: I suppose he just wanted to get a quick, **small pumping** or maybe a **good fuck**. Just the idea of going to a **whorehouse** would make me so nervous I wouldn't be able to **make it stand up**!

VOCABULARY

AIDS *m.* AIDS (an abbreviation for "Sindrome da immunodeficienza acquisita").

>   *example:* Massimo continua ad andare a puttane senza preservativo! Uno di questi giorni si beccherà l'**AIDS**.

>   *translation:* Massimo keeps going to prostitutes without using a condom! One of these days he's going to catch **AIDS**.

>   **NOTE:** It's interesting to note that in Italian, the abbreviation for *Sindrome da immunodeficienza acquisita* (AIDS) is backward and not SDIA as one would think!

baciare con la lingua *exp.* to French kiss • (lit.): to kiss with the tongue.

>   *example:* Sabato scorso Francesco è uscito con una sua compagna di classe e l'ha **baciata con la lingua** davanti al cinema.

>   *translation:* Last Saturday, Francesco went out with one of his classmates and **French kissed** her in front of the movie theater.

>   **SYNONYM 1:** **pomiciare** *v.* • (lit.): to pumice (from *pomice*, meaning "pumice stone" which is used by rubbing it against something else).

>   **SYNONYM 2:** **slinguare** *v.* • (lit.): to "tongue" (from the feminine noun *lingua*, meaning "tongue.")

bella scopata (una) *f.* a good lay, a good "boink" • (lit.): a good fuck.

> *example:*   Ieri sera Massimiliano è uscito con Patrizia; sono andati al cinema e poi hanno fatto **una bella scopata** sulla spiaggia.

> *translation:*   Last night, Massimiliano went out with Patrizia. They went to the movies and then had **a good boink** at the beach.

> **SYNONYM 1:**   **bombata** *f.* • (lit.): from the feminine noun *bomba*, meaning "bomb."

> **SYNONYM 2:**   **chiavata** *f.* • (lit.): from the feminine noun *chiave*, meaning "key," suggesting that the person can be easily "opened."

> **SYNONYM 3:**   **ciulata** *f.* (Northern Italy).

> **SYNONYM 4:**   **pigiata** *f.* • (lit.): from the verb *pigiare*, meaning "to push," suggesting that the person can be easily pushed into.

> **ALSO 1:**   **cosina veloce (una)** *f.* a quickie • (lit.): a quick little thing.

> **ALSO 2:**   **sveltina (una)** *f.* a quickie • (lit.): from the adjective *svelto/a*, meaning "quick."

bordello *m.* • **1.** brothel, whorehouse • **2.** big mess.

> *example 1:*   Tutti nel quartiere sono molto scontenti perchè hanno appena aperto un **bordello** vicino alla scuola!

> *translation:*   The neighborhood is very upset because a **brothel** just opened next to the school!

> *example 2:*   Raffaello non pulisce mai il suo appartamento. Non hai idea di come è dentro. Che **bordello**!

> *translation:*   Raffaello never cleans his apartment. You wouldn't believe what it looks like inside. What a **mess**!

> **SYNONYM 1:**   **casa chiusa** *f.* • (lit.): closed house.

> **SYNONYM 2:**   **casa di malaffare** *f.* • (lit.): house of bad/dirty business.

> **SYNONYM 3:**   **casa di tolleranza** *f.* • (lit.): house of tolerance.

> **SYNONYM 4:**   **casino** *m.*

SYNONYM 5:   **lupanare** m. (from the Latin word *lupa*, meaning "she wolf," which is slang for "prostitute").

SYNONYM 6:   **postribolo** m.

NOTE: Brothels are currently illegal in Italy. They were all shut down in the late 50s.

casino m. • **1.** brothel, a whorehouse • **2.** a big mess • **3.** an incredible loud noise.

   example 1:   L'anno scorso, quando Graziano è andato in Asia, è stato anche in un **casino** di Bangkok, dove tutte le puttane avevano meno di vent'anni.

   translation: Last year, when Graziano went to Asia, he also went to a **brothel** in Bangkok, where all the girls were under twenty.

   example 2:   Questa stanza è un gran **casino**! Ci sono carte e vestiti dappertutto!

   translation: This room is a big mess! There are papers and clothes everywhere!

   example 3:   Ieri sera, al concerto dei Backstreet Boys, tutti ballavano e gridavano; c'era un **casino** incredibile!

   translation: Last night at the Backstreet Boys concert, everyone danced and screamed; it was incredibly **noisy**!

SYNONYMS: See – **bordello**, *p. 68.*

farlo rizzare *exp.* to get it up, to make it hard, to have an erection • (lit.): to make it stand up.

   example: La prima volta che ho fatto sesso, non mi riusciva a **farlo rizzare**. Ero così nervoso!

   translation: The first time I had sex, I couldn't **get it up**. I was so nervous!

guanto m. condom • (lit.): glove.

   example: Oggigiorno se non ti metti il **guanto**, puoi avere guai!

   translation: Nowadays, if you don't wear a **rubber**, you could be in trouble!

SYNONYM 1:   **goldone** m. • (lit.): a gold coin that looks like a flat, unused condom.

SYNONYM 2:   **impermeabile** m. • (lit.): raincoat.

NOTE: A common mistake made by Americans is using the term *preservativo*, thinking it means "fruit preserves." Beware that *preservativo* means "condom" in everyday slang. Therefore, if you ask your waiter or waitress for some *preservativi* with your bread, you may get a strange look!

magnaccia *m.* pimp (from Roman *magnare,* a variation of the verb *mangiare,* meaning "to eat," i.e., "someone who eats with other people's money").

    example: Tutte quelle belle bionde che lavorano per il viale hanno un **magnaccia** che sta attento che loro non scappino.

    translation: All those beautiful blondes who work on the boulevard have a **pimp** who makes sure that they are not running away.

SYNONYM 1: **pappa/pappone** *m.* (from the verb *pappare,* meaning "to eat").

SYNONYM 2: **protettore** *m.* • (lit.): protector.

pompino *m.* blowjob • (lit.): a small pumping.

    example: Ho visto Flavia, in una macchina parcheggiata per strada, fare un **pompino** al suo ragazzo!

    translation: I saw Flavia giving a **blowjob** to her boyfriend in a car parked on the street!

SYNONYM 1: **bocchino** *m.* • (lit.): cigarette holder.

SYNONYM 2: **pipa (una)** *f.* • (lit.): a pipe (since it looks like the one giving the blowjob is smoking a pipe).

SYNONYM 3: **pompa (una)** *f.* • (lit.): a pump.

puttana *f.* • **1.** prostitute, whore • **2.** despicable woman, bitch.

    example: Hai visto quante **puttane** ci sono per strada stasera? Ci deve essere un gran giro di sesso in questo quartiere!

    translation: Did you see how many **prostitutes** are on the street tonight? Sex must be big business in this neighborhood!

SYNONYM 1: **bagascia** *f.*

SYNONYM 2: **battona** f. • (lit.): hitter (as in "one who hits the street" from the expression *battere la strada*, meaning "to walk the streets" or more literally "to hit the street").

SYNONYM 3: **maiala** f. • (lit.): female pig.

SYNONYM 4: **mignotta** f. *(Rome)* • (lit.): from the French word *mignonne*, meaning "cute little woman."

SYNONYM 5: **squillo** m. (from the verb *squillare*, meaning "to ring," i.e., call girl).

SNONYM 6: **troia** f. • (lit.): sow.

SYNONYM 7: **zoccola** f.

quartiere a luci rosse m. red-light district (where prostitution takes place) • (lit.): the quarter of red lights.

    example: Se andiamo ad Amsterdam, possiamo passare per il famoso **quartiere a luci rosse** per divertirci un po'!

    translation: If we go to Amsterdam, we could stop by the famous **red-light district** to have some fun!

troia f. prostitute • (lit.): sow.

    example: Ieri sera Giacomo è andato con una **troia** bellissima e molto giovane.

    translation: Last night, Giacomo took off with a beautiful and very young **prostitute**.

SYNONYMS: See – **puttana**, *p. 70.*

PRACTICE THE VOCABULARY

(Answers to Lesson Five, p. 177)

A. Match the English phrase in the left column with the Italian translation from the right. Write the appropriate letter in the box.

1. Last night, Giacomo took off with a beautiful and very young **prostitute**.

2. Massimo keeps seeing prostitutes and doesn't use a condom! One of these days he's going to get **AIDS**.

3. If we go to Amsterdam, we could stop by the famous **red-light district** to have some fun!

4. I saw Flavia giving a **blowjob** to her boyfriend in a car parked on the street!

5. The neighborhood is very upset because a **brothel** just opened next to the school!

6. Last Saturday, Francesco went out with one of his classmates and **French kissed** her in front of the movie theater.

7. The first time I had sex, I couldn't **get it up**. I was so nervous!

A. Sabato scorso Francesco è uscito con una sua compagna di classe e l'ha **baciata con la lingua** davanti al cinema.

B. Ieri sera Giacomo è andato con una **troia** bellissima e molto giovane.

C. La prima volta che ho fatto sesso, non mi riusciva a **farlo rizzare**. Ero così nervoso!

D. Se andiamo ad Amsterdam, possiamo passare per il famoso **quartiere a luci rosse** per divertirci un po'!

E. Raffaello non pulisce mai il suo appartamento. Non hai idea di come è dentro. Che **bordello**!

F. Massimo continua ad andare a puttane senza preservativo! Uno di questi giorni si beccherà l'**AIDS**.

G. Ho visto Flavia, in una macchina parcheggiata per strad,a fare un **pompino** al suo ragazzo.

B. Complete the opening dialogue by choosing the appropriate words from the list below. The English equivalents are in parentheses.

bordelli   **magnaccia**   **rosse**
farlo rizzare   **pompino**   **scopata**
guanto   **puttane**

Corrado: È una bellissima giornata! Che ne dici di fare due passi in centro?

Silvia: In centro? Ma è là dove c'è il quartiere a luci *(red)*_____!

È pieno di *(prostitutes)*_____,

*(pimps)*_____ e *(whorehouses)*_____!

Corrado: Lo so, ma è interessante da vedere. Sai, l'ultima volta che sono

passato da quelle parti, ho visto Fulvio con due troie. A dire il

vero, ne stava baciando una con la lingua.

Silvia: Be', se gli piacciono, spero che almeno usi un

*(rubber)*_____. Sono certa che non vuole

beccarsi l'AIDS.

Corrado: Immagino che voglia soltanto farsi fare un *(blowjob)*_____ ,

o fare magari una bella *(lay)*_____. Soltanto l'idea

di andare in un casino mi renderebbe così nervoso che non mi

riuscirebbe nemmeno *(to get it up)*_____!

C. Underline the correct definition.

1. **bella scopata (una):**
   a. a large penis
   b. a good lay

2. **bordello:**
   a. whorehouse
   b. whore

3. **casino:**
   a. whorehouse
   b. casino

4. **farlo rizzare:**
   a. to get it up, to get an erection
   b. to be impotent

5. **magnaccia:**
   a. someone who eats a lot
   b. pimp

6. **pompino:**
   a. an easy lay
   b. a blowjob

7. **puttana:**
   a. prostitute
   b. pimp

8. **quartiere a luci rosse:**
   a. whorehouse
   b. red-light district (where prostitution takes place)

9. **troia:**
   a. whorehouse
   b. prostitute

E. DICTATION
Test Your Listening Comprehension

(This dictation can be found in the Appendix on page 187.)

If you are following along with your cassette, you will now hear a series of sentences from the opening dialogue. These sentences will be read by a native speaker at normal conversational speed (which may seem fast to you at first). In addition, the words will be pronounced as you would actually hear them in a conversation, often including some common reductions.

The first time the sentences are presented, simply listen in order to get accustomed to the speed and heavy use of reductions. The sentences will then be read again with a pause after each to give you time to write down what you heard. The third time the sentences are read, follow along with what you have written.

REVIEW EXAM FOR LESSONS 1-5

(Answers to Review, p. 178)

A. Choose the correct definition of the words in boldface. Circle your answer.

1. **alito puzzolente:**
   a. bad breath
   b. pleasant breath

2. **allocco:**
   a. intelligent person
   b. stupid person

3. **amore a prima vista:**
   a. loves that ends in divorce
   b. love at first sight

4. **avere un chiodo fisso in testa:**
   a. to be fixated on someone/something
   b. to despise someone/something

5. **bagascia:**
   a. whore
   b. prostitute's client

6. **beccare qualcuno:**
   a. to dump someone
   b. to hit on someone

7. **bella scopata (una):**
   a. a large penis
   b. a good lay

8. **bellone:**
   a. a very handsome man
   b. a very ugly man

9. **bordello:**
   a. whorehouse
   b. whore

10. **casino:**
    a. whorehouse
    b. casino

11. **chiudere il becco:**
    a. to close one's mine to new ideas
    b. to shut one's mouth or "trap"

12. **donnaiolo:**
    a. a beautiful woman
    b. a womanizer

13. **essere un po'di fuori:**
    a. to be stood up on a date
    b. to be out of one's mind

14. **fare il galletto:**
    a. to flirt
    b. to get married

15. **fare il grande:**
    a. to show off
    b. to act like a big boy

16. **farlo rizzare:**
    a. to get it up, to get an erection
    b. to be impotent

17. **fesso/a:**
    a. stupid
    b. intelligent

18. **figlio di troia:**
    a. a good son
    b. son of a bitch

19. **fregarsene:**
    a. not to give a damn
    b. to care greatly

20. **grassone/a:**
    a. greasy
    b. a fatso

21. **guastafeste:**
    a. the life of the party
    b. a party pooper

22. **leccaculo:**
    a. brownnoser
    b. to have a large behind

23. **magnaccia:**
    a. someone who eats a lot
    b. pimp

24. **mostrare il dito medio:**
    a. to give the finger
    b. to thumb a ride

25. **portare male gli anni:**
    a. to age well
    b. not to age well

26. **rompiscatole:**
    a. a pain in the neck
    b. a very muscular man

27. **tirato/a:**
    a. pretty
    b. stingy

28. **Va'a farti fottere!:**
    a. How nice to see you again!
    b. Fuck you!

29. **Va'al diavolo!:**
    a. Hurry to the party!
    b. Go to hell!

B. Complete the phrases by choosing the best word from the list below.

anima	**fisso**	**spettegolare**
anni	**pelata**	**sporcaccioni**
bellone	**pigrone**	**torno**
bidone	**pornazzo**	**vista**
donnaioli	**schifoso**	

1. Non posso crederci! Massimo, il _____ che ho conosciuto la scorsa settimana, mi ha tirato un _____!

2. Credo che siano tutti dei _____ e che tutti abbiano quel chiodo _____ in testa.

3. Ed io poi sono così stanca di incontrare vecchi _____ che pensano che sia amore a prima _____ dopo cinque minuti!

4. Mi è proprio successo la scorsa settimana! Ma penso che quello volesse soltanto far sesso; per cui gli ho detto di levarsi di _____ e di andare invece a vedersi un bel _____!

5. Passa gran parte del giorno a _____ al telefono con i suoi amici. Quel tipo è un _____!

6. Certo, capisco cosa vuoi dire! Allora, hai assaggiato il cibo? È così _____! Pensavo addirittura di vomitare l'_____!

7. È cambiato così tanto! L'ultima volta che l'ho visto non aveva la zucca _____ come ora. A dire il vero porta davvero male gli _____!

C. Match the English phrase in the left column with the Italian translation from the right. Write the appropriate letter in the box.

☐ 1. This lasagna is **disgusting**! I think they made it with rotten meat!

☐ 2. Oreste is big **butt-kisser**! Every time he travels abroad, he brings back a little present for his math professor.

☐ 3. Yesterday evening, we were all ready to go dancing, but Filippo told us that he didn't want to take us there in his car. Filippo is really a **party pooper**!

☐ 4. I saw Flavia giving a **blowjob** to her boyfriend in a car parked on the street!

☐ 5. This party is really bad! **I'm bored to death**! Why don't we get out of here right now?

☐ 6. Armando is a **son of a bitch**! If I see him, I'm going to punch his lights out!

☐ 7. All those beautiful blondes who work on the boulevard have a **pimp** who makes sure that they are not running away.

☐ 8. The neighborhood is very upset because a **brothel** just opened next to the school!

A. Ho visto Flavia, in una macchina parcheggiata per strada, fare un **pompino** al suo ragazzo.

B. Tutte quelle belle bionde che lavorano per il viale hanno un **magnaccia** che sta attento che loro non scappino.

C. Tutti nel quartiere sono molto scontenti perchè hanno appena aperto un **bordello** vicino alla scuola!

D. Queste lasagne sono **schifose**! Credo che le abbiano fatte con della carne marcia!

E. Questa festa è veramente brutta! **Sto morendo dalla noia**! Perchè non ce ne andiamo subito?

F. Ieri sera eravamo tutti pronti per andare a ballare in discoteca, quando Filippo ci ha detto che non voleva accompagnarci in macchina. Filippo è proprio un **guastafeste**!

G. Oreste è un gran **leccaculo**! Tutte le volte che fa un viaggio all'estero, porta un regalino al professore di matematica.

H. Armando è un **figlio di troia**! Se lo vedo gli rompo la testa!

Credo che il tuo fratellino abbia appena *fatto un peto* in pubblico!

*(trans.): I think your little brother just **farted** in public!*
*(lit.): I think your little brother has just **done a fart** in public!*

Massimiliano: Prima che partiamo devo **fare un po'd'acqua**.

Edoardo: Sei sicuro? **Puzza da fare schifo** in quei **cessi**! Quel puzzo di **merda** mi fa venir voglia di **fare i gattini**! C'è sempre un gran tanfo di **sciolta** là dentro. Abbastanza da farti diventare subito **stitico**.

Massimiliano: Mi dispiace davvero dirtelo, ma credo che il tuo fratellino abbia appena **fatto un peto** in pubblico, o che **si sia cacato** nei pantaloni.

Edoardo: Nooo, Marchino! Di nuovo?

I think your little brother just *farted* in public!

Massimiliano: Before we leave, I need to **take a leak**.

Edoardo: Are you sure? It **stinks like crazy** in those **shit houses**! That smell of **shit** makes me want to **barf**! There's always a strong stench of **diarrhea** in there. It's enough to make you instantly **constipated**.

Massimiliano: I hate to tell you this, but I think your little brother either just **farted** in public or **took a dump** in his pants.

Edoardo: Nooo, Marchino! Again?

I think your little brother just *made a fart* in public!

Massimiliano:	Before we leave, I need to **make a little water**.
Edoardo:	Are you sure? It **stinks to disgust** in those **shit houses**! That smell of **shit** makes me want to **do little kittens**! There's always a strong stench of **melted** in there. It's enough to make you instantly **constipated**.
Massimiliano:	I hate to tell you this, but I think your little brother either just **made a fart** in public or **shit** in his pants.
Edoardo:	Nooo, Marchino! Again?

VOCABULARY

cacarsi nei pantaloni *exp.* to be scared shitless • (lit.): to shit in one's pants.

> *example:* Quando ho visto che quella macchina che accelerava verso di me, **mi sono cacato nei pantaloni**.
>
> *translation:* When I saw that car speeding toward me, **I was scared shitless**.

cesso *m.* (vulgar) public bathroom, "shithouse."

> *example:* Devo andare in bagno! C'è un **cesso** qui vicino?
>
> *translation:* I need to go to the bathroom. Is there a **shithouse** near here?
>
> **SYNONYM 1:** **cacatoio** *m.*
>
> **SYNONYM 2:** **pisciatoio** *m.* • (lit.): a pisser (from the verb *pisciare*, meaning "to piss").

fare i gattini *exp.* to barf, to vomit • (lit.): to make the kittens.

> *example:* Chiara ha mangiato qualcosa al ristorante che era andato a male e quando è tornata a casa ha **fatto i gattini**.
>
> *translation:* Chiara ate something at the restaurant that had turned bad and when she went back home, she **threw up**.

fare un peto *exp.* to fart • (lit.): to make a fart.

>   *example:* Dopo aver mangiato tutti quei fagioli, **farai peti** a
>   ripetizione!
>
>   *translation:* After eating all those beans, you're going **to fart** non-
>   stop!

SYNONYM 1:	**cureggiare** *v.*
SYNONYM 2:	**fare aria** *exp.* • (lit.): to make air.
SYNONYM 3:	**fare una cureggia** *exp.*
SYNONYM 4:	**fare una loffa** *exp.*
SYNONYM 5:	**fare una peta** *exp.* • (lit.): to make a fart.
SYNONYM 6:	**fare una puzza** *exp.* • (lit.): to make a stink.
SYNONYM 7:	**fare una scureggia** *exp.*
SYNONYM 8:	**loffare** *v.*
SYNONYM: 9	**petare** *v.* to fart.
SYNONYM 10:	**scureggiare** *v.*
VARIATION:	**scoreggiare** *v.*

fare un po'd'acqua *exp.* to take a leak, to urinate • (lit.): to make a
little water.

>   *example:* Scusatemi. Devo fare un salto in bagno a **fare un
>   po'd'acqua**.
>
>   *translation:* Excuse me. I need to run to the restroom **to take a
>   leak**.

SYNONYM 1:	**cambiare l'acqua al merlo/al passero** *exp.* • (lit.): to change the water to the blackbird/the sparrow.
SYNONYM 2:	**fare pipì** *exp.* • (lit.): to make pipi.
SYNONYM 3:	**pisciare** *v.* • (lit.): to piss.

merda *f.* • **1.** shit • **2.** a piece of shit (meaning "lousy") • (lit.): shit.

>   *example 1.* Stamani, mentre camminavo sul marciapiede, ho pe-
>   stato un'enorme **merda** di cane! Che puzzo!
>
>   *translation:* Earlier this morning, while I was walking along the
>   sidewalk, I stepped on a huge dog **shit**! Did it ever
>   stink!

example 2. Questo film è una **merda**!

translation: This is a shitty **movie**!

EUPHEMISM 1: **cacca** *m.* • (lit.): caca.

EUPHEMISM 2: **cagata** *f.* • (lit.): poop.

EUPHEMISM 3: **popò** *f.* • (lit.): poop, poo-poo.

puzzare da fare schifo *exp.* to stink to high heaven • (lit.): to smell/stink to disgust.

example: Mamma mia! Questo bagno **puzza da fare schifo**! Immagino che lo puliscano soltanto una volta al mese!

translation: Holy cow! This bathroom **smells to high heaven**! I guess they clean it only once a month!

SYNONYM: **puzzare da far vomitare** *exp.* • (lit.): to smell to make you vomit.

sciolta (la) *f.* the runs, diarrhea • (lit.): the melted.

example: Tommaso ha mangiato dieci chili di prugne ed ora ha **la sciolta**!

translation: Tommaso ate twenty pounds of prunes and now he has got **the runs**!

SYNONYM: **cacarella** *f.* • (lit.): the shits (from the verb *cacare*, meaning "to shit").

stitico/a *adj.* • **1.** constipated • **2.** stingy, tight with one's money.

example 1: Mario non mangia verdure da sei mesi! Probabilmente è **stitico**!

translation: Mario hasn't eaten vegetables for the past six months! He's probably **constipated**!

example 2: Mio nonno, quando vado a trovarlo, non mi dà mai soldi per compare un gelato. È davvero **stitico**!

translation: Whenever I visit my grandfather, he never gives me any money to buy ice cream. He's really **tight with money**!

PRACTICE THE VOCABULARY

(Answers to Lesson Six, p. 179)

A. Match the English phrase in the left column with the Italian translation from the right. Write the appropriate letter in the box.

☐ 1. Chiara ate something at the restaurant that had turned bad and when she went back home, she **threw up**.

☐ 2. Excuse me. I need to go quickly to the restroom **to take a leak**.

☐ 3. Earlier this morning, while I was walking along the sidewalk, I stepped on a huge dog **shit**! Did it ever stink!

☐ 4. I need to go to the bathroom. Is there a **shithouse** near here?

☐ 5. Whenever I visit my grandfather, he never gives me any money to buy ice cream. He's really **tight with money**!

☐ 6. Holy cow! This bathroom **smells to high heaven**! I guess that they clean it only once a month!

A. Devo andare in bagno! C'è un **cesso** qui vicino?

B. Chiara ha mangiato qualcosa al ristorante che era andato a male e quando è tornata a casa ha **fatto i gattini**.

C. Mio nonno, quando vado a trovarlo, non mi dà mai soldi per comprare un gelato. È davvero **stitico**!

D. Scusatemi. Devo fare un salto in bagno a **fare un po' d'acqua**.

E. Stamani, mentre camminavo sul marciapiede, ho pestato un'enorme **merda** di cane! Che puzzo!

F. Mamma mia! Questo bagno **puzza da fare schifo**! Immagino che lo puliscano soltanto una volta al mese!

B. Complete the opening dialogue by choosing the appropriate words from the list below. The English equivalents are in parentheses.

cessi   puzza da fare schifo

fare i gattini   sciolta

fare un po'd'acqua   si sia cacato

fatto un peto   stitico

merda

Massimiliano: Prima che partiamo devo *(to take a leak)* _____

_____.

Edoardo: Sei sicuro? *(It stinks to high heaven)*_____

_____ in quei

(shithouses) _____! Quel puzzo di *(shit)*

_____ mi fa venir voglia di *(barf my guts up)*

_____! C'è sempre un gran tanfo di

(the runs) _____ là dentro! Abbastanza da farti

diventare subito *(constipated)* _____!

Massimiliano: Mi dispiace davvero dirtelo, ma credo che il tuo fratellino

abbia appena *(farted)* _____ in

pubblico, o che *(took a shit)* _____ nei

pantaloni.

Edoardo: Nooo, Marchino! Di nuovo?

C. Underline the correct definition.

1. **cacarsi nei pantaloni:**
   a. to have diarrhea
   b. to be scared shitless

2. **cesso:**
   a. bathroom, "shithouse"
   b. prostitute

3. **fare i gattini:**
   a. to barf
   b. to have sex

4. **fare un peto:**
   a. to jilt someone
   b. to fart

5. **fare un po'd'acqua:**
   a. to have a drink
   b. to take a leak

6. **puzzare da fare schifo:**
   a. to have a slightly bad smell
   b. to stink to high heaven

7. **sciolta (la):**
   a. the runs
   b. a very hot day, a "scorcher"

8. **stitico/a:**
   a. stingy
   b. generous

9. **merda:**
   a. shit
   b. shoot

E. DICTATION
Test Your Listening Comprehension

(This dictation can be found in the Appendix on page 187.)

If you are following along with your cassette, you will now hear a series of sentences from the opening dialogue. These sentences will be read by a native speaker at normal conversational speed (which may seem fast to you at first). In addition, the words will be pronounced as you would actually hear them in a conversation, often including some common reductions.

The first time the sentences are presented, simply listen in order to get accustomed to the speed and heavy use of reductions. The sentences will then be read again with a pause after each to give you time to write down what you heard. The third time the sentences are read, follow along with what you have written.

Roberto ha una faccia di merda!

*(trans.): Roberto is as ugly as **shit**!*
*(lit.): Roberto has a **face of shit!***

LEZIONE SETTE · Dialogue in Slang

Costanza: La sai l'ultima? Roberto era fuori con un'altra tipa, quando per caso ha incontrato la sua ragazza!

Antonella: **Merda**! Roberto è il più gran **testone di merda** che abbia mai conosciuto! Ho sempre saputo che quella **merda** di Roberto prima o poi avrebbe **fatto una figura di merda** come quella. Sapevo anche che la sua storia con Angela sarebbe **finita in merda** un giorno o l'altro.

Costanza: Ho sempre saputo che era un **merdoso**, ma mai fino a quel punto! Chi mai vorrebbe uscire con uno che è così **pezzo di merda**? Non solo Roberto ha una gran **faccia di merda**, ma **puzza sempre di merda** e la sua casa è un gran **merdaio**!

Antonella: Sinceramente credo che la sua ragazza sia fortunata a mollare quello **merdaiolo** una volta per sempre!

Roberto is as ugly as shit!

Costanza: Did you hear the news? Roberto was on a date with some other girl when he ran into his girlfriend!

Antonella: **Shit**! Roberto's the biggest **idiot** I've ever known! I always knew, sooner or later, that **shithead** Roberto would **embarrass** himself like that. I also knew that relationship with Angelea would **go to shit** one of these days.

Costanza: I've always known he was a **shitty person**, but to that degree! Why would any guy want to go out with that **piece of shit**? Not only is Roberto **as ugly as shit**, but he always **smells like shit** and even his house is a total **shit hole**!

Antonella: Frankly, I think his girlfriend is lucky to be rid of that **shithead** once and for all!

Roberto has a *face of shit!*

Costanza: Did you hear the news? Roberto was on a date with some other girl when he ran into his girlfriend!

Antonella: **Shit**! He's is the biggest **head of shit** I've ever known! I always knew, sooner or later, that **shit** Roberto would **make a figure of shit** like that. I also knew that relationship with Angela would **finish in shit** one of these days.

Costanza: I've always known he was a **shitty person**, but to that point! Why would any girl want to go out with that **piece of shit**? Not only does Roberto have a **face of shit**, but he always **smells like shit** and even his house is a total **shitty and filthy place**!

Antonella: Frankly, I think his girlfriend is lucky to be rid of that **person who is full of shit** once and for all!

VOCABULARY

di merda *adv.* lousy, shitty • (lit.): of shit.

    example: Ieri sera siamo stati ad una festa **di merda**! C'erano pochissime ragazze e quelle che erano lì erano bruttissime; il cibo e la musica poi erano terribili!

    translation: Last night, we went to a **shitty** party! There were only a few girls, and the ones who were there were actually very ugly. The food and the music then were just terrible!

    SYNONYM: **del cazzo** *adv.* • (lit.): of the dick.

faccia di merda *f.* a very despicable person, an asshole, a bastard, a son of a bitch • (lit.): a face of shit.

    example: Augusto ha proprio una gran **faccia di merda**! Tutte le volte che vede la mia ragazza, fa qualche commento stronzo sui suoi vestiti.

    translation: Augusto is really a **bastard**! Every single time he sees my girlfriend, he's got some nasty comment to make about her clothes.

    SYNONYM 1: **faccia di cazzo** *f.* • (lit.): dick face.

    SYNONYM 2: **faccia di ciola** *f.*

    SYNONYM 3: **faccia di stronzo** *f.* • (lit.): turd head.

fare una figura di merda *exp.* to make a shitty impression, to embarrass oneself • (lit.): to make a figure of shit.

    example: Franco ieri sera **ha fatto una figura di merda** alla festa di Costanza. Ha offeso davanti a tutti la sua ex ragazza!

    translation: Last night, Franco really **made a shitty impression** at Costanza's party. He offended his ex-girlfriend in front of everyone!

SYNONYM 1:   **fare una brutta/bruttissima figura** *exp.* • (lit.): to make an ugly/very ugly figure.

SYNONYM 2:   **fare una figura da imbecille** *exp.* • (lit.): to make a figure of imbecile.

SYNONYM 3:   **fare una figura da scemo/a** *exp.* • (lit.): to make a figure as a stupid person.

SYNONYM 4:   **fare una figura del cazzo** *exp.* • (lit.): to make a figure of the penis or "dick."

finire in merda *exp.* to end miserably • (lit.): to end in shit.

example: La storia fra Luigi e Sara è **finita in merda**, dopo che Sara lo ha trovato a letto con un'altra.

translation: The relationship between Luigi and Sara **ended miserably** after Sara found him in bed with another woman.

merda *f. & adj.* shit, shitty, a piece of shit, mean son of a bitch.

example: Corrado qualche volta è davvero una **merda**; gli ho chiesto di prestarmi la sua macchina e lui ha detto no!

translation: Sometimes Corrado is really a **shit**. I asked him if I could borrow his car and he said no!

"Merda!" *interj.* • (lit.): "Shit!"

example: **Merda**! Ho perso l'autobus!

translation: **Shit**! I missed the bus!

merdaio (un) *m.* a very dirty and disgusting place, a shit hole • (lit.): a place full of shit.

example: L'appartamento di Franco e Gabriele è un **merdaio**! C'è sporco dappertutto, puzza e il bagno fa schifo!

translation: Franco and Gabriele's apartment is a **shit hole**! It's filthy everywhere, it smells, and the bathroom is disgusting!

merdaiolo/a *n.* shit, despicable person, bitch.

> *example:* Quella **merdaiola** mi ha appena tamponato! Guarda come mi ha ridotto la macchina!
>
> *translation:* That **bitch** just rear-ended me! Look what she did to my car!

merdoso/a *adj.* a very despicable person, a shitty person, an asshole • (lit.): a shitty one.

> *example:* Che **merdoso**, Giovanni! Tratta sempre male la sua ragazza quando escono insieme il fine settimana.
>
> *translation:* Giovanni is such an **asshole**! He always treats his girl-friend badly when they go out together on weekends.

SYNONYM 1: **figlio di puttana** *m.* • (lit.): son of whore.

SYNONYM 2: **merda (una)** *f.* • (lit.): a shit.

SYNONYM 3: **stronzo/a** *n.* • (lit.): turd.

pezzo di merda *m.* a despicable person, a bastard • (lit.): piece of shit.

> *example:* **Pezzo di merda**! Restituiscimi subito la borsa o chiamo la polizia e ti faccio arrestare!
>
> *translation:* **You bastard**! Give me back my purse right away, or I'll call the police and have you arrested!

SYNONYMS: See – **merdoso/a**, *p. 99.*

testone/a di merda *n.* a fucking idiot • (lit.): big head of shit.

> *example:* Marco è un gran **testone di merda**. È sempre nei guai e non mi dà mai retta.
>
> *translation:* Marco is a **fucking idiot**. He's always in trouble and never follows my advise.

SYNONYM 1: **fessacchione/a** *n.* • (lit.): big idiot.

SYNONYM 2: **imbecillone/a** *n.* • (lit.): big imbecile.

SYNONYM 3: **stronzone/a** *n.* • (lit.): big turd.

SYNONYM 4: **stupidone/a** *n.* • (lit.): big idiot.

PRACTICE THE VOCABULARY

(Answers to Lesson Seven, p. 180)

A. Match the English phrase in the left column with the Italian translation from the right. Write the appropriate letter in the box.

1. That **bitch** just rear-ended me! Look what she did to my car!

2. Sometimes Corrado is really a **shit**. I asked him if I could borrow his car and he said no!

3. **You bastard**! Give me back my purse right away, or I'll call the police and have you arrested!

4. Franco and Gabriele's apartment is a **shit hole**! It's filthy everywhere!

5. Marco is a **fucking idiot**. He's always in trouble and never follows my advise.

6. The relationship between Luigi and Sara **ended miserably**, after Sara found him in bed with another woman.

A. Marco è un gran **testone di merda**. È sempre nei guai e non mi dà mai retta.

B. Corrado qualche volta è davvero una **merda**; gli ho chiesto di prestarmi la sua macchina e lui ha detto no!

C. Quella **merdaiola** mi ha appena tamponato! Guarda come mi ha ridotto la macchina!

D. **Pezzo di merda**! Restituiscimi subito la borsa o chiamo la polizia e ti faccio arrestare!

E. L'appartamento di Franco e Gabriele è un **merdaio**! C'è sporco dappertutto!

F. La storia fra Luigi e Sara è **finita in merda**, dopo che Sara lo ha trovato a letto con un'altra.

B. Complete the opening dialogue by choosing the appropriate words from the list below. The English equivalents are in parentheses.

faccia
fatto una figura di merda
finita in merda
merda
merdaio

merdoso
pezzo di merda
puzza sempre di merda
testone di merda

Costanza: La sai l'ultima? Roberto era fuori con un'altra tipa, quando per

caso ha incontrato la sua ragazza!

Antonella: (Shit)_____ ! Roberto è il più gran (shithead)

_____ che abbia mai conosciuto!

Ho sempre saputo che quella merda di Roberto prima o poi

avrebbe (embarrassed) _____

come quella. Sapevo anche che la sua storia con Angela sarebbe

(to end miserably) _____ un giorno o

l'altro.

Costanza: Ho sempre saputo che era un (very despicable person)

_____, ma mai fino a quel punto! Chi mai

vorrebbe uscire con uno che è così (piece of shit)

_____? Non solo Roberto ha una

(face)_____ di merda, ma (he always stinks like shit)

_____ e la sua casa è un gran (dirty and disgusting

place) _____!

Antonella: Sinceramente credo che la sua ragazza sia fortunata a mollare

quello merdaiolo una volta per sempre!

C. Underline the correct definition.

1. **di merda:**
   a. lousy, shitty
   b. dirty

2. **faccia di merda:**
   a. a very despicable person
   b. a very dirty face

3. **fare una figura di merda:**
   a. to gain weight
   b. to make a bad impression

4. **finire in merda:**
   a. to end miserably
   b. to end successfully

5. **merdaio (un):**
   a. a lucky person
   b. a very dirty and disgusting place

6. **merdaiolo/a:**
   a. a very dirty and disgusting place
   b. a despicable or "shitty" person

7. **merdoso/a:**
   a. a despicable or "shitty" person
   b. an ugly person

8. **testone/a di merda:**
   a. a big idiot
   b. a genius

9. **pezzo di merda:**
   a. a despicable person, a "piece of shit"
   b. junk

E. DICTATION
Test Your Listening Comprehension

(This dictation can be found in the Appendix on page 188.)

If you are following along with your cassette, you will now hear a series of sentences from the opening dialogue. These sentences will be read by a native speaker at normal conversational speed (which may seem fast to you at first). In addition, the words will be pronounced as you would actually hear them in a conversation, often including some common reductions.

The first time the sentences are presented, simply listen in order to get accustomed to the speed and heavy use of reductions. The sentences will then be read again with a pause after each to give you time to write down what you heard. The third time the sentences are read, follow along with what you have written.

Mi sono cagato addosso dalla paura!

(trans.): I was **scared shitless**!
(lit.): I **shit on myself for fear**!

Giorgio: Ieri notte sono stato scippato alla metro. Mi **sono cagato addosso dalla paura**!

Filippo: Stai scherzando? Che è successo?

Giorgio: Beh, mi era venuta voglia di **fare una cagata** e così mi ero messo a cercare un **cacatoio**. Quando sono entrato, c'era un altro tizio che **cagava**. Immagino che avesse **la cacarella**, o qualcosa di simile, perchè quel posto puzzava da morire! Comunque, mi sono infilato nel cesso accanto al suo. Quando sono uscito, c'erano due omoni là fuori che aspettavano; sembravano tosti e dei gran **cacasodo**. Di solito io non sono un **cacasotto**, ma ho avuto subito l'impressione che ci sarebbero stati guai. All'improvviso, il più **cacasenno** dei due, mi guarda in faccia e mi dice di dargli l'orologio. Beh, in quel momento non mi sono sentito in vena di fare nè il **cacasentenze** nè il **cacamiracoli** e così, gliel'ho dato. Oltre tutto il mio orologio non valeva un gran chè. Era una **cagata** che comprai anni fa. Quando poi mi ha detto di allungargli tutti i miei soldi, gli ho risposto che non ne avevo. Allora lui mi ha **mandato a cagare** e ha cominciato a rincorrermi!

Filippo: Mamma mia! Mi sarei **cagato nei pantaloni** anch'io!

I was
scared shitless!

Giorgio: Last night, I was robbed in the subway. I was **scared shitless**!

Filippo: Are you joking? What happened?

Giorgio: Well, I needed to **take a shit** so I went to look for a **shithouse**. When I walked in, there was another guy in there who was **taking a shit**. He must have had **diarrhea** or something because it really stunk in there! Anyway, I went into the stall next to him. When I came out, there were two big men standing there waiting who seemed like **tough guys**. I'm not usually a **scaredy cat** but I had the feeling right away that there was going to be trouble. All of a sudden, the bigger **smart-ass** of the two looks me right in the face and tells me to give him my watch. Well, at that moment I didn't feel that it was appropriate to act like **one who moralizes** or **hesitates**, so I just gave it to him. Besides, my watch wasn't worth very much. It was an old **piece of shit** I bought years ago. Then when he told me to hand him all my money, I told him that I didn't have any. So, he **told me to fuck off** and started running after me!

Filippo: Wow! I would have been **scared shitless**, too!

I shit on myself for fear!

Giorgio: Last night, I was robbed in the subway. I **shitted** on myself for fear!

Filippo: Are you joking? What happened?

Giorgio: Well, I needed to **make a shit** so I went to look for a **place where one shits**. When I walked in, there was another guy in there who was **shitting**. He must have had **the shits** or something because the place really stunk to death! Anyway, I went into the stall next to him. When I came out, there were two big guys standing there waiting who seemed like **big, hard shitters**. I'm not usually a **one who shits on himself** but I had the feeling right away that there was going to be trouble. All of a sudden, the more **shit-wise** of the two looks at me right in the face and tells me to give him my watch. Well, at that moment I didn't feel that it was appropriate to act like a **judgement-shitter** or **one who shits miracles**, so I just gave it to him. Besides, my watch wasn't worth very much. It was an old **piece of shit** I bought years ago. Then when he told me to hand him all my money, I told him that I didn't have any. So, he **sent me to shit** and started running after me!

Filippo: Wow! I would have **shitted in my pants**, too!

VOCABULARY

cacamiracoli (un/una) *n.* someone who takes a lot of time, makes a lot of difficulties before giving up/granting something, a stingy person • (lit.): one who shits miracles.

      example: Roberto è un gran **cacamiracoli**! Tutte le volte che lo prego di prestarmi la sua macchina per un paio d'ore, fa un sacco di storie!

    translation: Roberto is a very **stingy person**! Everytime I ask him to lend me his car for a couple of hours, he makes such a fuss!

cacarella *f.* • (lit.): the shits (from the verb *cacare*, meaning "to shit").

      example: Dopo aver mangiato della carne schifosa, ieri, ho avuto la **cacarella** per tre giorni!

    translation: After eating some bad meat yesterday, I had **the runs** for three days!

cacasenno (un/una) *n.* a know-it-all, a smart-ass • (lit.): one who shits wisdom.

      example: Giulio è proprio un **cacasenno**! Crede di sapere tutto, ma in realtà non sa un cazzo!

    translation: Giulio is really a **smart-ass**! He thinks he knows everything, but he actually doesn't know shit!

    SYNONYM 1: **cacasentenze (un/una)** *n.* • (lit.): moral shitter.

    SYNONYM 2: **saccente (un/una)** *n.* • (lit.): from the verb *sapere*, meaning "to know."

    SYNONYM 3: **saputo un/una saputa** *n.* • (lit.): from the verb *sapere*, meaning "to know."

    SYNONYM 4: **sputasentenze (un/una)** *n.* • (lit.): moral spitter.

cacasentenze (un/una) *n.* one who likes to moralize; one who acts like he/she is very smart, a smart-ass • (lit.): one who shits sentences.

> *example:* Marco è un **cacasentenze** con tutti; anche con i suoi genitori! In realtà però non credo che abbia idea di quello che dice!

> *translation:* Marco is a **smart-ass** with everybody, even with his parents! But I truly don't think he has a clue about what he's saying!

cacasodo (un/una) *n.* an arrogant person, someone who thinks his/her shit doesn't stink • (lit.): one who takes a hard shit (from the verb *cacare*, meaning "to shit" and the adjective *sodo/a*, meaning "tough" or "hard").

> *example:* Quel buttafuori è un gran **cacasodo**. Si comporta come se fosse il padrone del locale.

> *translation:* That bouncer **thinks his shit doesn't shink**. He acts as if he were the owner of the club.

cacasotto (un/una) *n.* a very fearful person, a "chicken-shit" • (lit): one who shits down below.

> *example:* Serena è davvero una **cacasotto**! Non ha mai il coraggio di entrare in quel vecchio cimitero abbandonato, di notte.

> *translation:* Serena is really a **chicken-shit**! She never has the guts to walk into that old abandoned cemetery at night.

cacatoio *m.* (very vulgar) the "shithouse," the "crapper," a place where one takes a shit • (lit.): shitter (from the verb *cacare*, meaning "to shit").

> *example:* Se non trovo subito un **cacatoio** pubblico, mi cagherò addosso!

> *translation:* If I don't find a **crapper** immediately, I'm going to shit in my pants!

> **SYNONYM:** **cesso** *m.*

cagare/cacare *v.* to defecate • (lit.): to shit.

> *example:* Giuseppe deve aver appena **cagato**. Nel bagno non si respira!

translation: Giuseppe must have just **taken a shit**. You can't breathe in the bathroom!

SYNONYM: See – **fare una cagata/cacata**, *p. 112.*

ALSO: **andare a cagare** *interj.* to fuck off • (lit): to go shit • *Va'a cagare!;* Fuck off!/Fuck you!

cagarsi/cacarsi addosso dalla paura *exp.* to be scared shitless
• (lit.): to shit on oneself for fear.

example: Quando ho visto la polizia che sparava a pochi metri da me, **mi sono cagato/cacato addosso dalla paura**!

translation: When I saw the police shooting a few feet from where I was standing, I **was scared shitless**!

SYNONYM 1: **farsela sotto dalla paura** *exp.* • (lit.): to make it down below on oneself for fear.

SYNONYM 2: **pisciarsi addosso dalla paura** *exp.* • (lit.): to pee on oneself for fear.

cagarsi/cacarsi nei pantaloni *exp.* to be scared shitless • (lit.): to shit in one's pants.

example: Quando il rapinatore mi ha puntato la pistola in faccia, **mi sono cagato nei pantaloni**!

translation: When the robber pointed the gun in my face, I **was shitting in my pants**!

SYNONYM: **farsela nei pantaloni** *exp.* • (lit.): to do it in one's pants.

cagata/cacata (una) *f.* bullshit, something worthless, a piece of shit • (lit.): a shit.

example: Quest'orologio che ho comprato l'anno scorso per due soldi, è proprio una **cagata**!

translation: This watch I bought last year for a few bucks is really a **piece of crap**!

SYNONYM 1: **boiata (una)** *f.* • (lit.): from the masculine noun *boia,* meaning "executer."

SYNONYM 2: **cazzata (una)** *f.* • (lit.): from the masculine noun *cazzo,* meaning "penis" or "dick."

SYNONYM 3: **cretinata (una)** *f.* • (lit.): from the adjective *cretino/a,* meaning "cretin."

SYNONYM 4: **fesseria (una)** *f.* • (lit.): from the masculine noun *fesso,* meaning "crack."

SYNONYM 5: **merdata (una)** *f.* • (lit.): from the feminine noun *merda,* meaning "shit."

SYNONYM 6: **puttanata (una)** *f.* • (lit.): from the feminine noun *puttana,* meaning "whore."

SYNONYM 7: **stronzata (una)** *f.* • (lit.): from the mascuine noun *stronzo,* meaning "turd."

SYNONYM 8: **stupidaggine (una)** *f.* • (lit.): from the adjective *stupido/a,* meaning "stupid."

fare una cagata/cacata *exp.* to take a shit • (lit.): to make a shit.

example: Ho mangiato così tanto che ho davvero bisogno di **fare una cagata/cacata**!

translation: I ate so much that now I really need **to take a shit**!

SYNONYM 1: **andare di corpo** *exp.* • (lit.): to go with one's body.

SYNONYM 2: **cagare/cacare** *v.* • (lit.): to defecate.

SYNONYM 3: **fare la merda** *exp.* • (lit.): to make shit.

SYNONYM 4: **fare la poppò/popò** *exp.* (euphemism) • (lit.): to go poopoo.

mandare a cagare/cacare qualcuno *exp.* to tell someone to fuck off • (lit.): to send someone to shit.

example: Quando il mio inquilino mi ha detto che non poteva pagare questo mese, l'ho **mandato a cagare**!

translation: When my tenant told me that he could't pay me this month, I told him **to fuck off**!

SYNONYM 1: **mandare qualcuno a fanculo** *exp.*

SYNONYM 2: **mandare qualcuno a fantasca** *exp.* • (lit.): to send someone to do in the pocket.

SYNONYM 3: **mandare qualcuno a quel paese** *exp.* • (lit.): to send someone to that country.

SYNONYM 4: **mandare qualcuno al diavolo** *exp.* • (lit.): to send someone to the devil.

PRACTICE THE VOCABULARY

(Answers to Lesson Eight, p. 181)

A. Match the English phrase in the left column with the Italian translation from the right. Write the appropriate letter in the box.

1. That bouncer **thinks his shit doesn't shink**. He acts as if he were the owner of the club.

2. This watch that I bought last year for a few bucks is really a **piece of crap**!

3. Serena is really a **chicken-shit**! She never has the guts to walk into that old abandoned cemetery at night.

4. When I saw the police shooting a few feet from where I was standing, I **was scared shitless**!

5. When my tenant told me that he couldn't pay me this month, I told him **to fuck off**!

6. Marco is a **smart-ass** with everybody, even with his parents! But I truly don't think he has a clue about what he's saying!

A. Marco è un **cacasentenze** con tutti; anche con i suoi genitori! In realtà però non credo che abbia idea di quello che dice!

B. Quando ho visto la polizia che sparava a pochi metri da me, **mi sono cagato/cacato addosso dalla paura**!

C. Quando il mio inquilino mi ha detto che non poteva pagare questo mese, l'ho **mandato a cagare**.

D. Quest'orologio che ho comprato l'anno scorso per due soldi, è proprio una **cagata**!

E. Serena è davvero una **cacasotto**! Non ha mai il coraggio di entrare in quel vecchio cimitero abbandonato, di notte.

F. Quel buttafuori è un gran **cacasodo**. Si comporta come se fosse il padrone del locale.

B. Complete the following phrases by choosing the appropriate words from the list below.

cacamiracoli   cacarella
cacasenno   cagare
cacasentenze   cagata
cacasodo   cagato
cacasotto   cagava
cacatoio   fare una cagata

Giorgio: Ieri notte sono stato scippato alla metro. Mi sono _____
            addosso dalla paura!

Filippo: Stai scherzando? Che è successo?

Giorgio: Beh, mi era venuta voglia di _____e così
            mi ero messo a cercare un _____. Quando sono
            entrato c'era un altro tizio che _____. Immagino che
            avesse la _____ qualcosa di simile, perchè quel
            posto puzzava da morire! Comunque mi sono infilato nel cesso
            accanto al suo. Quando sono uscito c'erano due omoni là fuori
            che aspettavano; sembravano tosti e dei gran
            _____. Di solito io non sono un _____,
            ma ho avuto subito l'impressione che ci sarebbero stati guai.
            All'improvviso, il più _____ dei due, mi guarda
            in faccia e mi dice di dargli l'orologio. Beh, in quel momento non
            mi sono sentito in vena di fare nè il _____
            nè il _____ e così, gliel'ho dato. Oltre tutto il
            mio orologio non valeva un gran chè. Era una _____
            che comprai anni fa. Quando poi mi ha detto di allungargli tutti i
            miei soldi, gli ho risposto che non ne avevo. Allora lui mi ha
            mandato a _____ e ha cominciato a rincorrermi!

Filippo: Mamma mia! Mi sarei cagato nei pantaloni anch'io!

C. Underline the correct definition.

1. **cacamiracoli (un/una):**
   a. a stingy person
   b. a crazy person

2. **cacasenno (un/una):**
   a. a beautiful person
   b. a know-it-all, a smart-ass

3. **cacasodo (un/una):**
   a. an arrogant person
   b. a funny person

4. **cacasotto (un/una):**
   a. a fearful person, a "chicken-shit"
   b. a very brave person

5. **cacatoio:**
   a. a shitty person
   b. bathroom, "shithouse"

6. **cagare/cacare:**
   a. to be scared shitless
   b. to defecate, to shit

7. **cagarsi/cacarsi addosso dalla paura:**
   a. to be very brave
   b. to be scared shitless

8. **cagata/cacata (una):**
   a. something worthless
   b. something valuable

9. **mandare a cagare/cacare qualcuno:**
   a. to make love to someone
   b. to tell someone to go fuck off

E. DICTATION
Test Your Listening Comprehension

(This dictation can be found in the Appendix on page 188.)

If you are following along with your cassette, you will now hear a series of sentences from the opening dialogue. These sentences will be read by a native speaker at normal conversational speed (which may seem fast to you at first). In addition, the words will be pronounced as you would actually hear them in a conversation, often including some common reductions.

The first time the sentences are presented, simply listen in order to get accustomed to the speed and heavy use of reductions. The sentences will then be read again with a pause after each to give you time to write down what you heard. The third time the sentences are read, follow along with what you have written.

Francesco non è altro che una gran *testa di cazzo*.

*(trans.): Francesco is nothing but a big **dickhead**!*
*(lit.): Francesco is nothing but a big **head of dick**!*

LEZIONE NOVE · Dialogue in Slang

Gabriele: Come vanno le cose con il tuo ospite?

Franco: Da fare schifo! Francesco non solo è una gran **testa di cazzo**, ma anche il più grande **fancazzista** che abbia mai conosciuto. Non **fa mai un cazzo** in casa. Non fa che guardare questi spettacoli televisivi **del cazzo** tutto il giorno. Ma la cosa che **mi fa incazzare** di più, sono tutte quelle **cazzate** che racconta. Ho l'impressione che si inventi tutto per far colpo sulla gente. **Che figura del cazzo**! La cosa peggiore poi, è che **non si fa mai i cazzi suoi**.

Gabriele: **Cazzo**! È proprio un **cazzone**!

Franco: Fortunatamente se ne andrà fra un paio di giorni. Oh, no! È proprio lui e viene verso di noi! Chissà che **cazzo vuole**? Guarda come guida **alla cazzo**! Sta guidando sul marciapiede! Spostati!

Francesco is a big *dickhead!*

Gabriele: How is everything going with your houseguest?

Franco: It's horrible! Francesco is not only a big **dickhead**, but also the biggest **lazy bum** I've ever met. He **never does a thing** around the house. He just watches these **jerky** TV shows all day. But the thing that **pisses me off** the most are all those **bullshit stories** he tells. I get the feeling he makes things up to impress people. **It's really embarrassing**! But the worst is that he **doesn't mind his own business**.

Gabriele: **Shit**! He's really a **prick**!

Franco: Luckily, he's leaving in two days. Oh, no! That's him coming toward us! I wonder **what the hell he wants**. He even drives **like an idiot**! He's driving on the sidewalk! Move!

Francesco is a big *head of dick!*

Gabriele: How is everything going with your houseguest?

Franco: It's horrible! Francesco is not only a big **head of dick**, but also the biggest **dick-doer** I've ever met. He **never does a dick** around the house. He just watches these **dick-like** TV shows all day. But the thing that **makes me get into my dick** the most are all those **dick-like** stories he tells. I get the feeling he makes things up to impress people. **What a figure of the dick**! But the worst is that he **doesn't do his own dicks**.

Gabriele: **Dick**! He's really a **big dick**!

Franco: Luckily, he's leaving in two days. Oh, no! That's him driving toward us! I wonder **what dick he wants**. Look how he drives **dick-style**! He's driving on the sidewalk! Move!

VOCABULARY

alla cazzo *adv.* said of something done in an idiotic way • (lit.): in the manner of the dick, dick-like.

    example: Quella vecchietta guida proprio **alla cazzo**! Se non fa attenzione andrà a battere contro quel palo!

    translation: That little old lady drives **like a jerk**! If she doesn't pay attention, she's going to hit that pole!

    VARIATION: **alla cazzo di cane** *adv.* • (lit.): in the manner of a dog's dick.

    SYNONYM: **alla boia** *adv.* • (lit.): in the manner of the executioner.

cazzata (una) *f.* • **1.** bullshit • **2.** something worthless, a piece of shit.

    example 1:   Quello che dici è una **cazzata**! Non è vero che Carlotta ed io usciamo insieme.

    translation: What you're saying is **bullshit**! It's not true that Carlotta and I are going out together.

    example 2:   Questo bell'orologio che ho comprato ieri si è già fermato! Che **cazzata**!

    translation: This beautiful watch I bought yesterday already stopped! What a **piece of shit**!

    SYNONYM 1:   **bischerata (una)** *f.* (Tuscan) • (lit.): from the masculine noun *bischero*, meaning "penis."

    SYNONYM 2:   **cavolata (una)** *f.* • (lit.): from the masculine noun *cavolo*, meaning "cabbage."

    SYNONYM 3:   **cosa da niente (una)** *f.* • (lit.): a thing of nothing.

    SYNONYM 4:   **fesseria (una)** *f.* • (lit.): from the noun *fesso*, meaning "crack."

    SYNONYM 5:   **puttanata (una)** *f.* • (lit.): from the feminine noun *puttana*, meaning "whore."

SYNONYM 6:   **scemata (una)** f. • (lit.): from the verb *scemare,*
meaning "to shrink."

"Cazzo!" *interj.* "Damn!" or "Shit!" • (lit.): "Dick!"

example: **Cazzo**! Se non mi muovo, perdo l'autobus!

translation: **Damn**! If I don't get moving, I'm going to miss the bus!

SYNONYM 1:   **"Figa!"** *interj.* (an extremely vulgar term for "vagina")
"Pussy!"

SYNONYM 2:   **"Merda!"** *interj.* • (lit.): "Shit!"

cazzo (del) *adv.* worthless, of bad quality, shitty (when used to modify a
noun) • (lit.): of the dick.

example: È stato proprio un concerto **del cazzo**! Le canzoni
erano bruttissime e non cantavano nemmeno dal vivo!

translation: It truly was a **shitty** concert! The songs were really
bad and they didn't even play live!

cazzo (un) *m.* nothing, zip • (lit.): a dick.

example 1:   –C'è qualcosa da mangiare stasera?
–No, **non c'è un cazzo** in frigo!

translation: –Is there anything to eat tonight?
–No, **there's shit** in the refrigerator!

example 2:   Gino **non sa un cazzo** di macchine!

translation: Gino **doesn't know shit** about cars!

SYNONYM 1:   **accidente (un)** m. • (lit.): an accident.

SYNONYM 2:   **bel niente (un)** m. • (lit.): a beautiful nothing.

SYNONYM 3:   **mazza (una)** f. (very vulgar) • (lit.): a stick.

SYNONYM 4:   **sega (una)** f. (very vulgar) • (lit.): a saw.

cazzone/a *n.* a very stupid person, a "dickhead" • (lit.): a big dick.

example: Alberto è proprio un **cazzone**. Non capisce mai le
barzellette che gli raccontiamo. Dobbiamo sempre
spiegargliele.

translation: Alberto is a real **dickhead**. He never get the jokes we tell him. We always have to explain them to him.

SYNONYMS: See – **fesso/a**, *p. 55.*

"Che cazzo vuole?" *exp.* "What the fuck does he/she want?" • (lit.): "What dick does he/she want?"

example: **Che cazzo vuole**? Perchè non smette di suonarmi? Non vede che sta guidando contro mano?

translation: **What the hell does he want**? Why doesn't he stop honking at me? Doesn't he realize that he's driving the wrong way?

SYNONYM: **"Che cavolo vuole?"** *exp.* (euphemism) • (lit.): "What cabbage does he/she want?"

"Che figura del cazzo!" *interj.* "How embarrassing!" • (lit.): "What a figure of the dick!"

example: Mario è tornato a casa ieri sera e sua moglie ha subito notato che aveva dei signi di rossetto sul collo e sulla bocca! **Che figura del cazzo**!

translation: Mario got back home last night and right away his wife noticed some lipstick marks on his neck and mouth! **How embarrassing**!

SYNONYM: **"Che figura di merda!"** *interj.* • (lit.): "What a figure of shit!"

fancazzista *n.* a lazy bum, a "lazy sack of shit" • (lit.): dick doer (from the expression *fare un cazzo*, literally meaning "to do a dick").

example: Armando è un gran **fancazzista**! Lo hanno assunto la settimana scorsa e sta tutto il giorno a scrivere messaggi elettronici ai suoi amici.

translation: Armando is a **lazy sack of shit**. They hired him last week and he spends the whole day writing email to his friends!

SYNONYM 1: **fannullone/a** *n.* • (lit.): do-nothing (from *fare nulla*, meaning "to do nothing."

SYNONYM 2: **pigrone/a** *n.* • (lit.): a big lazy bum.

farsi i cazzi propri *exp.* to mind one's own business • (lit.): to make one's own dicks.

> *example:* Paolo non **si fa mai i cazzi suoi**. Prima o poi si caccerà in qualche guaio serio!
>
> *translation:* Paolo **never minds his own business**. Sooner or later, he's going to get in some serious trouble!
>
> **SYNONYM:** **farsi gli affari propri** *exp.* • (lit.): to make one's own affairs.

fare incazzare qualcuno *exp.* to piss someone off.

> *example:* Gianna **mi fa sempre incazzare**. Tutte le volte che le chiedo se vuol mettersi con me, mi dice che non è pronta.
>
> *translation:* Gianna **always pisses me off**. Every time I ask her if she wants to be my girlfriend, she answers that she's not ready.
>
> **SYNONYM 1:** **fare arrabbiare qualcuno** *exp.*
>
> **SYNONYM 2:** **fare incavolare qualcuno** *exp.* (euphemism) • (lit.): to turn someone into cabbage.
>
> **SYNONYM 3:** **mandare qualcuno in bestia** *exp.* • (lit.): to send someone to the beast.

testa di cazzo *f.* a despicable person, an asshole• (lit.): dickhead.

> *example:* Simone è una **testa di cazzo**! Guida sempre come un pazzo, e uno di questi giorni la polizia lo fermerà e gli farà una multa pazzesca!
>
> *translation:* Simone is an **asshole**! He always drives like a mad person, and one of these days the police are going to stop him and give him a huge ticket!
>
> **SYNONYM 1:** **coglione/a** *n.* • (lit.): testicle.
>
> **SYNONYM 2:** **cretino/a** *n.* • (lit.): cretin.
>
> **SYNONYM 3:** **fava** *m.* • (lit.): fava bean.
>
> **SYNONYM 4:** **imbecille** *n. & adj.* • (lit.): imbecile.

PRACTICE THE VOCABULARY

(Answers to Lesson Nine, p. 182)

A. Match the English phrase in the left column with the Italian translation from the right. Write the appropriate letter in the box.

☐ 1. It was really a **shitty** concert. The songs were really bad and they didn't even play live!

☐ 2. **What the hell does he want**? Why doesn't he stop honking at me? Doesn't he realize that he's driving the wrong way?

☐ 3. Simone is an **asshole**! He always drives like a wacko. One of these days the police are going to stop him and give him a huge ticket!

☐ 4. –Is there anything to eat tonight?
–No, **there's shit** in the refrigerator!

☐ 5. Paolo **never minds his own business**. Sooner or later, he's going to get in some serious trouble!

☐ 6. Gianna **always pisses me off**. Every time I ask her if she wants to be my girlfriend, she answers that she's not ready.

A. Simone è una **testa di cazzo**! Guida sempre come un pazzo. Uno di questi giorni la polizia lo fermerà e gli farà una multa pazzesca!

B. Paolo non **si fa mai i cazzi suoi**. Prima o poi si caccerà in qualche guaio serio!

C. –C'è qualcosa da mangiare stasera?
–No, **non c'è un cazzo** in frigo!

D. È stato proprio un concerto **del cazzo**. Le canzoni erano bruttissime e non cantavano nemmeno dal vivo!

E. **Che cazzo vuole**? Perchè non smette di suonarmi? Non vede che sta guidando contro mano?

F. Gianna **mi fa sempre incazzare**. Tutte le volte che le chiedo se vuol mettersi con me, mi dice che non è pronta.

B. Complete the opening dialogue by choosing the appropriate words from the list below. The English equivalents are in parentheses.

alla cazzo   del cazzo
cazzate   fa mai un cazzo
cazzo   fancazzista
cazzo vuole   mi fa incazzare
cazzone   non si fa mai i cazzi suoi
che figura del cazzo   testa di cazzo

Gabriele: Come vanno le cose con il tuo ospite?

Franco: Da fare schifo! Francesco non solo è una gran *(dickhead)*

_____, ma anche il più grande *(lazy bum)*

_____ che abbia mai conosciuto. Non

(never does "dick" around the house) _____

_____ in casa. Non fa che guardare questi

spettacoli televisivi *(shitty)* _____ tutto il giorno.

Ma la cosa che *(pissed me off)* _____ di più, sono

tutte quelle *(bullshit)* _____ che racconta. Ho

l'impressione che si inventi tutto per far colpo sulla gente. *(How

embarrassing)*_____! La cosa peggiore

poi, è che *(never minds his own business)*

_____.

Gabriele: *(Damn)*_____! È proprio un *(big idiot)*_____!

Franco: Fortunatamente se ne andrà fra un paio di giorni. Oh, no! È

proprio lui e viene verso di noi! Chissà che *(the hell does he want)*

_____? Guarda come guida *(like an

idiot)*_____! Sta guidando sul marciapiede!

Spostati!

C. Underline the correct definition.

1. **alla cazzo:**
   a. something done in an idiotic way
   b. something done in a clever way

2. **cazzata (una):**
   a. bullshit / something worthless
   b. an ugly person

3. **cazzo (un):**
   a. nothing, "zip"
   b. a beautiful face

4. **cazzo (del):**
   a. said of something expensive
   b. said of something worthless

5. **cazzone/a:**
   a. a smart person
   b. a stupid person, a "dickhead"

6. **"Che cazzo vuole?":**
   a. "What the fuck does he/she want?"
   b. "What can I do for you?"

7. **"Che figura del cazzo!":**
   a. "How wonderful!"
   b. "How embarrassing!"

8. **fancazzista:**
   a. a very helpful person
   b. a lazy bum, a lazy "piece of shit"

9. **fare incazzare qualcuno:**
   a. to piss someone off
   b. to thrill someone

E. DICTATION
Test Your Listening Comprehension

(This dictation can be found in the Appendix on page 189.)

If you are following along with your cassette, you will now hear a series of sentences from the opening dialogue. These sentences will be read by a native speaker at normal conversational speed (which may seem fast to you at first). In addition, the words will be pronounced as you would actually hear them in a conversation, often including some common reductions.

The first time the sentences are presented, simply listen in order to get accustomed to the speed and heavy use of reductions. The sentences will then be read again with a pause after each to give you time to write down what you heard. The third time the sentences are read, follow along with what you have written.

Che culo!

*(trans.): What **luck**!*
*(lit.): What **an ass**!*

LEZIONE DIECI · Dialogue in Slang

Federico: Arianna! **Che culo**! Sono così contento di averti trovata. Non crederai a quello che è successo oggi. Conosci la proprietaria del negozio all'angolo?

Arianna: Vuoi dire quella **culona** che **lecca il culo a tutti**?

Federico: No, no! Non la **leccaculo**. Quella è la commessa. Parlo invece della proprietaria; quella con quel bel **culino** e quella terribile **faccia di culo**. Bene, oggi ho visto un tipo che le gridava in faccia, perchè lei glielo ha **messo in culo** e ha cercato anche di farlo pagare! E lui continuava a gridare: "Questa è un'**inculata**!"

Arianna: Lo capisco, poveretto. Anch'io l'ho **preso in culo** da lei! Quella cerca sempre di aggiungere qualche lira alla tua carta di credito.

Federico: Bene, lei si è così arrabbiata con lui per averle gridato in faccia, che ha cominciato a **prenderlo per il culo**. Alla fine poi gli ha anche detto **vaffanculo**! Ho davvero pensato che lei poi saltasse di là dal bancone e gli **facesse il culo**!

Che *culo!*

Federico: Arianna! **What luck**! I'm so glad I found you. You won't believe what happened today. You know that woman who owns the store on the corner?

Arianna: You mean the one with the **fat ass** who **kisses up to everyone**?

Federico: No, no! Not the **ass-kisser**. That's the salesperson. I'm talking about the owner; the one with the **small ass** and **butt-ugly**. Well, today I saw some guy screaming at her because she **cheated him** and tried to charge him three times the price! He just kept screaming, "This is a **rip-off**!"

Arianna: I don't blame him, poor guy. I was **ripped off** by her before, too! She always tries to add extra money onto your credit card.

Federico: Well, she got so mad at him for yelling at her that she started **making fun of him**. Finally, she told him to **fuck off**! I really thought she was going to jump over the counter and **kick his ass**!

What an ass!

Federico: Arianna! **What an ass**! I'm so glad I found you. You won't believe what happened today. You know that woman who owns the store on the corner?

Arianna: You mean the **big-assed woman** who **licks everyone's ass**?

Federico: No, no! Not the **ass-licker**. That's the salesperson. I'm talking about the owner; the one with the **small ass** and **face of butt**. Well, today I saw some guy screaming in her face because she **put it in his ass** and tried to charge him three times the price! He just kept screaming, "This is a **butt-fucking**!"

Arianna: I understand him, poor guy. I **took it in ass** by her before, too! That one always tries to add extra money onto your credit card.

Federico: Well, she got so mad at him for yelling at her that she started **taking him from the ass**. At the end, she also told him to **go do it in the ass**! I really thought she was going to jump over the counter and **do his ass**!

VOCABULARY

"Che culo!" *interj.* "What luck!" • (lit.): "What an ass!"

 example: **Che culo**! Stefania ha vinto alla lotteria!

 translation: **What luck**! Stefania won the lottery!

 NOTE: This interjection is somewhat vulgar, yet extremely common among younger people.

 SYNONYM 1: **"Che mele!"** *interj.* • (lit.): "What apples!"

 NOTE: *Mele*, literally "apples," is slang for one's rear end.

 SYNONYM 2: **"Che paiolo!"** *interj.* • (lit.): "What a copper pot!"

 NOTE: *Paiolo*, literally "a copper pot," is slang for one's rear end.

culone/a *n.* one with a big, fat ass (from the masculine noun *culo*, meaning "ass").

 example: Quella **culona** di Federica vuole uscire con me, ma io non voglio nemmeno pensarci!

 translation: That **fat ass** Federica wants to go out with me, but I don't even want to think about it!

culino *m.* a small ass (from the masculine noun *culo*, meaning "ass").

 example: Sara ha proprio un bel **culino**! E guarda come lo muove!

 translation: Sara really has a cute **little butt**! And look how she moves it!

 SYNONYM 1: **culetto** *m.* • (lit.): little buttocks.

 SYNONYM 2: **meline** *m.* • (lit.): small apples (from the feminine noun *mela*, meaning "apple").

 SYNONYM 3: **sederino** *m.* • (lit.): "sitter" (from the verb *sedere*, meaning "to sit").

faccia di culo *f.* • **1.** a butt-ugly face • **2.** used as an insult, referring to a big jerk (lit.): face of ass.

> *example 1:* Matteo ha proprio una **faccia di culo**! Non so come farà a trovar moglie!
>
> *translation:* Matteo really has a **butt-ugly face**! I wonder how he'll get married!
>
> *example 2:* Fermati, **faccia di culo**! Non vedi che il semaforo è rosso?
>
> *translation:* Stop, **you fucking idiot**! Don't you see that the light is red?
>
> **SYNONYM 1:** **faccia di cazzo** *f.* • (lit.): dickface.
>
> **SYNONYM 2:** **faccia di merda** *f.* • (lit.): shitface.

fare il culo a qualcuno *exp.* to kick somebody's ass • (lit.): to make the ass to somebody.

> *example:* Ehi, tu! Se non lasci stare la mia ragazza, vengo lì e ti **faccio il culo**!
>
> *translation:* Hey, you! If you don't leave my girlfriend alone, I'm going to come over there and **kick your butt**!
>
> **SYNONYM:** **fare la festa a qualcuno** *exp.* • (lit.): to do the party to somebody.
>
> **ALSO:** **farsi il culo** *exp.* to work hard towards a goal, to work one's butt off • (lit.): to do one's butt • *Mi sono fatto il culo per quasi due mesi a studiare, e ho superato l'esame brillantemente!;* I worked my butt off studying for two months and passed the exam with flying colors!
>
> > **NOTE:** A common Italian expression using both *fare il culo* and *farsi il culo* is: *O ti fai il culo, o te la fanno!;* You either work your butt off or they will kick your butt!

inculata *f.* (very vulgar) a rip-off • (lit.): a butt-fucking.

> *example:* Che **inculata** ieri sera al ristorante! Abbiamo mangiato malissimo ed il conto era da non crederci!
>
> *translation:* What a **rip-off** last night at the restaurant! The food was really awful and the bill was unbelievable!
>
> **SYNONYM 1:** **fregatura** *f.* • (lit.): a rubbing.

SYNONYM 2:	**inchiappettata** *f.* • (lit.): to get it between the buttocks (from the feminine plural noun *chiappe*, meaning "buttocks").

leccaculo *n.* butt-kisser, brownnoser • (lit.): ass-licker.

> *example:* Quella **leccaculo** di Francesca otterrà sempre ciò che vuole!
>
> *translation:* That **butt-kisser** Francesca will get anything she wants!

SYNONYM 1:	**leccapiedi** *m.* • (lit.): foot-licker.
SYNONYM 2:	**lecchino/a** *n.* • (lit.): licker.
SYNONYM 3:	**ruffiano/a** *n.*

leccare il culo a qualcuno *exp.* to butt kiss • (lit.): to lick someone's ass.

> *example:* Giacomo vuole un bel voto nel corso di filosofia e per ottenerlo non fa che **leccare il culo al professore**.
>
> *translation:* Giacomo wants a good grade in his philosophy class, and in order to get it, he does nothing but **kiss his professor's butt**.

SYNONYM 1:	**fare il ruffiano/la ruffiana con qualcuno** *exp.* • (lit.): to make the pimp with someone.
SYNONYM 2:	**leccare i piedi a qualcuno** *exp.* • (lit.): to lick someone's feet.

metterlo in culo a qualcuno *exp.* (extremely vulgar) to cheat someone, to rip someone off • (lit.): to put it in someone's ass, to buttfuck someone.

> *example:* La commessa di quel negozietto **me lo ha messo nel culo** ieri pomeriggio! Non mi ha dato i venti Euro di resto. Mi ha dato soltanto la metà del resto che mi doveva!
>
> *translation:* The saleswoman in that small store **cheated me** yesterday afternoon! She didn't give me the Euros back in change. She gave me only half the change she was supposed to give me!

SYNONYM 1:	**fregare qualcuno** *v.* • (lit.): to rub someone.
SYNONYM 2:	**inculare qualcuno** *v.* • (lit.): to buttfuck someone.

prenderlo in culo da qualcuno *exp.* (very vulgar) • **1.** to get cheated, to get ripped off • **2.** to get beaten up by someone • (lit.): to get it in the ass by someone.

> *example:* La scorsa settimana **lo abbiamo preso nel culo** da quella concessionaria. Ci hanno venduto una macchina usata schifosa!
>
> *translation:* Last week, **we were cheated** by those car dealers. They sold us a worthless, used car!

SYNONYM 1: **farsi fregare da qualcuno** *exp.*

SYNONYM 2: **farsi inculare da qualcuno** *exp.* • (lit.): to get oneself butt-fucked by someone.

SYNONYM 3: **prenderlo nelle mele da qualcuno** *exp.* • (lit.): to take it between the apples (meaning "buttocks").

prendere per il culo qualcuno *exp.* to make fun of someone, to pull someone's leg • (lit.): to get someone by the ass.

> *example:* Luca è un po' lento. Tutti lo **prendono per il culo** e lui nemmeno se ne accorge!
>
> *translation:* Luca is a bit slow. Everybody's **making fun of** him and he doesn't even get it!

SYNONYM 1: **fare fesso qualcuno** *exp.* • (lit.): to make someone stupid.

SYNONYM 2: **prendere in giro qualcuno** *exp.* • (lit.): to take someone in circle.

SYNONYM 3: **prendere qualcuno per il bavero** *exp.* (Tuscan) • (lit.): to take someone by the collar.

SYNONYM 4: **prendere qualcuno per le fondelli** *exp.* (Tuscan) • (lit.): to take someone from the bottoms (used to mean "buttocks").

SYNONYM 5: **prendere qualcuno per le mele** *exp.* (Tuscan) • (lit.): to take someone by the apples (used to mean "buttocks").

"Vaffanculo!" *interj.* "Fuck off!" "Fuck you!" • (lit.): "Go do in the ass!" (short for *"Va'a fare in culo!"*).

> *example:* Ehi! **Vaffanculo**! Quel posto è mio! Se non te ne vai subito esco di macchina e te le do!
>
> *translation:* Hey, you! **Fuck off**! That was my spot! If you don't leave right away, I'm going to get out of my car and kick your butt!

PRACTICE THE VOCABULARY

(Answers to Lesson Ten, p. 183)

A. Match the English phrase in the left column with the Italian translation from the right. Write the appropriate letter in the box.

□ 1. Last week **we were cheated** by those car dealers. They sold us a worthless, used car!

□ 2. Giacomo wants a good grade in his philosophy class, and in order to get it, he does nothing but **kiss his professor's butt**.

□ 3. Hey, you! **Fuck off**! That was my parking spot! If you don't leave right away, I'm going to get out of my car and kick your butt!

□ 4. The salewoman in that small store **cheated me** yesterday afternoon! She didn't give me the Euros back in change. She gave me only half the change she was supposed to give me!

□ 5. Luca is a bit slow. Everybody's **making fun of** him and he doesn't even get it.

□ 6. That **butt-kisser** Francesca will always get what she wants!

A. Ehi! **Vaffanculo**! Quel posto è mio! Se non te ne vai subito esco di macchina e te le do!

B. Luca è un po'lento! Tutti lo **prendono per il culo** e lui nemmeno se ne accorge!

C. La scorsa settimana **lo abbiamo preso nel culo** da quella concessionaria. Ci hanno venduto una macchina usata schifosa!

D. La commessa di quel negozietto **me lo ha messo nel culo** ieri pomeriggio! Non mi ha data i venti Euro di resto. Mi ha dato soltanto la metà del resto che mi doveva!

E. Giacomo vuole un bel voto nel corso di filosofia e per ottenerlo non fa che **leccare il culo al professore**.

F. Quella **leccaculo** di Francesca otterrà sempre ciò che vuole!

B. Complete the opening dialogue by choosing the appropriate words from the list below. The English equivalents are in parentheses.

che culo
culino
culo
culona
faccia di culo
facesse il culo

inculata
leccaculo
messo in culo
prenderlo per il culo
vaffanculo

Federico: Arianna! *(What luck)* _____! Sono così contento di
               averti trovata. Non crederai a quello che è successo oggi!
               Conosci la proprietaria del negozio all'angolo?

Arianna: Vuoi dire quella *(fat ass)* _____ che lecca il *(ass)*
               _____ a tutti?

Federico: No, no! Non la *(butt-kisser)* _____. Quella è la
               commessa. Invece mi riferisco alla proprietaria; quella con quel
               bel *(little butt)* _____ e quella terribile *(butt-ugly*
               face) _____. Bene, oggi ho visto un
               tipo che le gridava in faccia, perchè lei glielo ha *(cheated)*
               _____ e ha cercato anche di farlo pagare! E lui
               continuava a gridare: "Questa è un'*(rip-off)*_____!"

Arianna: Lo capisco, poveretto. Anch'io l'ho preso in culo da lei! Quella
               cerca sempre di aggiungere qualche lira alla tua carta di credito.

Federico: Bene, lei si è così arrabbiata con lui per averle gridato in faccia,
               che ha cominciato a *(make fun of him)* _____
               _____ e alla fine poi gli ha anche detto *(fuck off)*
               _____! Ho davvero pensato che lei poi saltasse
               di là dal bancone e gli *(kick his ass)* _____!

C. Underline the correct definition.

1. **"Che culo!":**
    a. "What a big ass!"
    b. "What luck!"

2. **culone/a:**
    a. one with a fat ass
    b. one with a little ass

3. **culino:**
    a. a fat ass
    b. a little ass

4. **faccia di culo:**
    a. a beautiful face
    b. a butt-ugly face

5. **fare il culo a qualcuno:**
    a. to show off
    b. to kick someone's ass

6. **inculata:**
    a. a bargain
    b. a rip-off

7. **leccaculo:**
    a. butt-kisser
    b. boss

8. **prendere per il culo qualcuno:**
    a. to talk a lot to someone
    b. to make fun of someone

9. **metterlo in culo a qualcuno:**
    a. to give someone a friendly slap on the buttocks
    b. to cheat someone

10. **"Vaffanculo!":**
    a. "Fuck off!"
    b. "How nice to see you!"

E. DICTATION
Test Your Listening Comprehension

(This dictation can be found in the Appendix on page 189.)

If you are following along with your cassette, you will now hear a series of sentences from the opening dialogue. These sentences will be read by a native speaker at normal conversational speed (which may seem fast to you at first). In addition, the words will be pronounced as you would actually hear them in a conversation, often including some common reductions.

The first time the sentences are presented, simply listen in order to get accustomed to the speed and heavy use of reductions. The sentences will then be read again with a pause after each to give you time to write down what you heard. The third time the sentences are read, follow along with what you have written.

REVIEW EXAM FOR LESSONS 6-10

(Answers to Review, p. 184)

A. Choose the correct definition of the words in boldface. Circle your answer.

1. **bagascia:**
   a. whore
   b. prostitute's client

2. **bella scopata (una):**
   a. a large penis
   b. a good lay

3. **bordello:**
   a. whorehouse
   b. whore

4. **cacarsi nei pantaloni:**
   a. to have diarrhea
   b. to be scared shitless

5. **casino:**
   a. whorehouse
   b. casino

6. **cesso:**
   a. bathroom, "shithouse"
   b. prostitute

7. **di merda:**
   a. lousy, shitty
   b. dirty

8. **essere un po'di fuori:**
   a. to be stood up on a date
   b. to be out of one's mind

9. **faccia di merda:**
   a. a very despicable person
   b. a very dirty face

10. **fare i gattini:**
    a. to barf
    b. to have sex

11. **fare un peto:**
    a. to jilt someone
    b. to fart

12. **fare un po'd'acqua:**
    a. to have a drink
    b. to take a leak

13. **fare una figura di merda:**
    a. to gain weight
    b. to make a bad impression

14. **farlo rizzare:**
    a. to get it up, to get an erection
    b. to be impotent

15. **fesso/a:**
    a. stupid
    b. intelligent

16. **figlio di troia:**
    a. a good son
    b. son of a bitch

17. **finire in merda:**
    a. to end miserably
    b. to end successfully

18. **grassone/a:**
    a. greasy
    b. a fatso

19. **guastafeste:**
    a. the life of the party
    b. a party pooper

20. **leccaculo:**
   a. brownnoser
   b. to have a large behind

21. **magnaccia:**
   a. someone who eats a lot
   b. pimp

22. **merdaio (un):**
   a. a lucky person
   b. a very dirty and disgusting place

23. **mostrare il dito medio:**
   a. to give the finger
   b. to thumb a ride

24. **portare male gli anni:**
   a. to age well
   b. not to age well

25. **puzzare da fare schifo:**
   a. to have a slightly bad smell
   b. to stink to high heaven

26. **rompiscatole:**
   a. a pain in the neck
   b. a very muscular man

27. **Va'a farti fottere!:**
   a. How nice to see you again!
   b. Fuck you!

28. **Va'al diavolo!:**
   a. Hurry to the party!
   b. Go to hell!

B. Fill in the blanks with the word that best completes the phrase.

alla cazzo	**finita in merda**
cazzo vuole	**fatto un peto**
che culo	**merda**
fare un po'd'acqua	**si sia cacato**
fatto una figura di merda	**testona di merda**

1. Arianna! *(What luck)* _____! Sono così contento di averti trovata. Non crederai a quello che è successo oggi. Conosci la proprietaria del negozio all'angolo?

2. Fortunatamente se ne andrà fra un paio di giorni. Oh, no! È proprio lui e viene verso di noi! Chissà che *(what the hell does he want)* _____? Guarda come guida *(like an idiot)*_____! Sta guidando sul marciapiede! Spostati!

3. *(Shit)*_____ ! Roberta è la più grande *(shithead)* _____ che abbia mai conosciuto! Ho sempre saputo che quella merda di Roberta prima o poi avrebbe *(embarrassed)* _____ come quella. Sapevo anche che la sua storia con Maurizio sarebbe *(to end miserably)* _____ un giorno o l'altro.

4. Prima che partiamo devo *(to take a leak)* _____ _____.

5. Mi dispiace davvero dirtelo, ma credo che il tuo fratellino abbia appena *(farted)* _____ in pubblico, o che *(took a shit)* _____ nei pantaloni.

C. Match the English phrase in the left column with the Italian translation from the right. Write the appropriate letter in the box.

1. That little old lady drives **like a jerk**! If she doesn't pay attention, she's going to hit that pole!

2. When my tenant told me that he couldn't pay me this month, I told him **to fuck off**!

3. Last week, **we were cheated** by those car dealers. They sold us a worthless, used car!

4. When I saw the police shooting a few feet from where I was standing, I **was scared shitless**!

5. Gianna **always pisses me off**. Every time I ask her if she wants to be my girlfriend, she answers that she's not ready.

6. The relationship between Luigi and Sara **ended miserably** after Sara found him in bed with another woman.

7. Sara really has a cute **little butt**! And look how she moves it!

8. Last night, Franco really **made a shitty impression** at Costanza's party. He offended his ex-girlfriend in front of everyone!

A. Sara ha proprio un bel **culino**! E guarda come lo muove!

B. Gianna **mi fa sempre incazzare**. Tutte le volte che le chiedo se vuol mettersi con me, mi dice che non è pronta.

C. Quella vecchietta guida proprio **alla cazzo**! Se non fa attenzione andrà a battere contro quel palo!

D. Quando il mio inquilino mi ha detto che non poteva pagare questo mese, l'ho **mandato a cagare**.

E. Quando ho visto la polizia che sparava a pochi metri da me, **mi sono cagato/cacato addosso dalla paura**!

F. La storia fra Luigi e Sara è **finita in merda**, dopo che Sara lo ha trovato a lettto con un'altra.

G. La scorsa settimana **lo abbiamo preso nel culo** da quella concessionaria. Ci hanno venduto una macchina usata schifosa!

H. Franco ieri sera **ha fatto una figura di merda** alla festa di Costanza. Ha offeso davanti a tutti la sua ex ragazza!

STREET ITALIAN 2

PART 2

GESTURES

"WHAT DO YOU WANT FROM ME?"

*The tips of the fingers of one hand are brought together
and either held motionless or waved forward and back.*

---

example: Angela, fra noi è davvero finita! Ma che
vuoi da me?

translation: Angela, it's through between us! What do
you want from me?

"WANNA GET A DRINK?"

Use your thumb as if it were the spout of a bottle and pantomime pouring liquid into your mouth.

---

example: Che dici, ce la facciamo una bevutina?

translation: What do you say we get a little something to drink?

"WHAT ARE YOU? NUTS?"

*The tips of the fingers point downward
as you hit your forehead with a limp hand.*

---

example: Tu sei tutto matto se credi che quella abbia
intenzione di uscire con te!

translation: You're out of your mind if you think she'd
go out with you!

VARIATION: Tap the temple of your head several times.

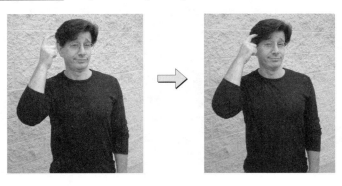

"I'M FURIOUS!"

The knuckle of one of your fists is put in your mouth as you pantomime biting it. This can also be accompanied by a growl like an angry dog.

---

example: Non riesco a credere che mi hai graffiato la macchina!

translation: I can't believe you scratched my car!

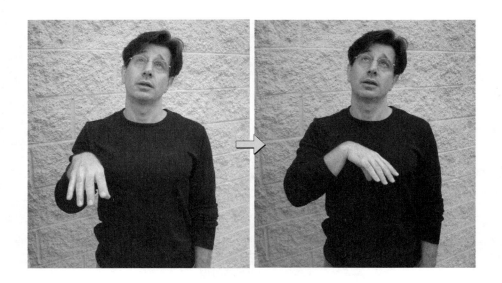

"THIS IS SO BORING!"

The tips of the fingers point downward
as you hit your chest with a limp hand.

---

example: Mamma mia! Che lezione noiosa!
translation: Man, oh man! What a boring lesson!

VARIATION: Pantomime having a long beard.

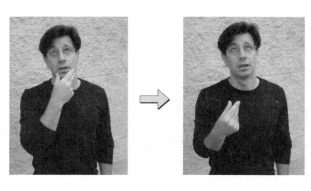

"THEY'RE REALLY GETTING ALONG!"

The two index fingers are rubbed
together back and forth several times.

---

example: Quei due vanno davvero d'accordo, eh?

translation: Those two are certainly getting along great,
huh?

"CUCKOLD!"

Show your hand with your little finger and index finger pointing upward, like horns. With this gesture, you have the option of keeping your hand faced forward or backward.

---

example: Ma che moglie hai? Mi sembra che tu abbia più corna in testa che un cesto pieno di lumache!

translation: What kind of wife do you have? You are more cuckold than you can imagine!

NOTE: The word for "cuckold" in Italian is *cornuto*, literally meaning "with horns." Therefore, the literal translation of the example sentence above becomes: "It looks like you have more horns than a basket full of snails!"

"EVERYTHING IS GOING GREAT!"

This gesture is the same as the American gesture for "okay." But beware! This same gesture in Brazil means "You asshole!"

---

example: – Come va oggi?
            – Tutto a posto, grazie!

translation: – How's it going today?
            – Perfectly well, thanks!

NOTE: **tutto a posto** *exp.* • (lit.): everything is in place.

"WAIT!"

*Simply push your entire hand forward toward the
person you're addressing. But beware! This same
gesture in Greece is extremely insulting!*

---

example: Aspetta un momento! Giù le mani, Fabio!

translation: Just a moment! Get your hands down,
              Fabio!

"GET WHAT I'M SAYING?"

Use your index finger to pull down the lower lid of your eye. By the way, this same gesture in France means "That's a bunch of baloney!"

---

example: Stasera portiamo al ristorante quelle due francesi, poi ce ne andiamo tutti in spiaggia! Inteso?

translation: Tonight, we're taking two French girls to a restaurant, then we're all going to the beach! Get what I'm saying?

"IT WAS STOLEN!"

The hand is open with the fingers stretched out. Starting with the little finger, each finger is slowly brought down as if grabbing something.

---

example: Quella cassiera trova sempre un modo per fregarmi un po' di spiccioli!

translation: That cashier always finds a way to steal a little change from me!

"YOU'RE GONNA GET IT!"

*Use the back of your thumb and run it across the front of
your throat, as if you were slashing it with a knife.*

---

example: Se non te ne vai subito di qua, sai cosa ti
           aspetta!

translation: If you don't get out of here right away, you
           know what you're in for!

VARIATION: Make a cross toward the other person.

"I COULDN'T CARE LESS!"

*The back of the fingers rub under
the chin and fly forward.*

---

example: Chi se ne frega se Luciana mi ha lasciato!
Ne troverò un'altra!

translation: Who cares if Luciana dumped me! I'll find
someone else!

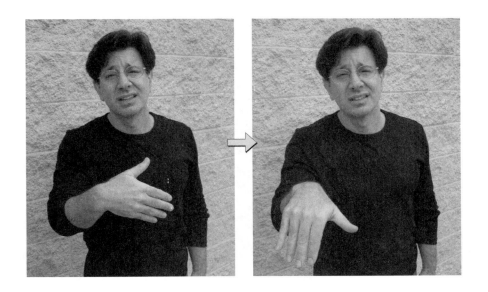

"BEAT IT!"

The back of the hand faces the person you're addressing as you swing your hand back and forth.

---

    example: Scappa, prima che ti metta le mani addosso!

translation: Beat it before I knock your block off!

VARIATION: Give several karate chops to the palm of the other hand.

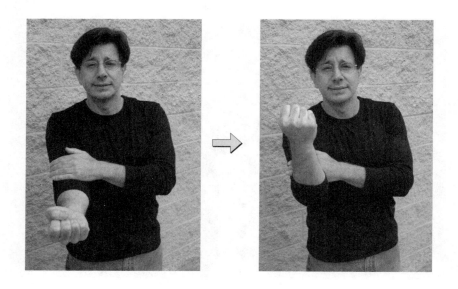

"UP YOURS!"

*The hand of one arm covers the bicep of the other
arm which is extended while holding a fist.
The fist is then jerked up quickly.*

---

example: Questo è per averci provato con la mia
ragazza!

translation: This is for trying to hit on my girlfriend!

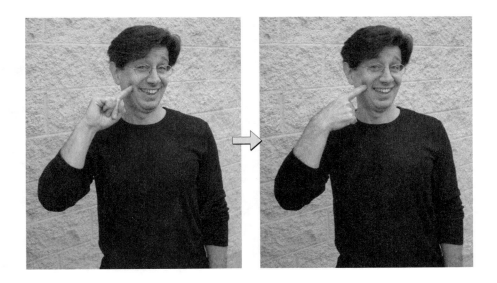

"DELICIOUS!"

Twist the tip of the index finger back and forth against your cheek.

---

example: Mamma mia! Che bocconcino è quella ragazza là!

translation: Wow! What a tasty little morsel she is!

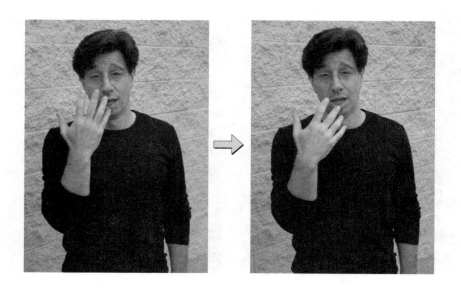

"WHAT A DOPE!"

Strum your lower lip several times like a guitar,
starting with your little finger.

---

example: Filippo non ne azzecca mai una agli esami.
Deve mancargli qualche rotella in testa!

translation: Filippo doesn't get a single question right
on the exams. I think he's kind of a dope!

NOTE: **mancare qualche rotella in testa a
qualcuno** *exp.* to be missing one's
marbles • (lit.): to miss some wheels in
one's head.

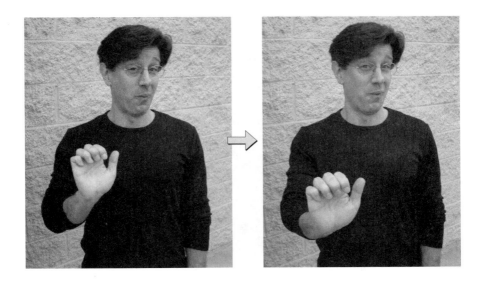

"THEY'RE GETTING IT ON BIG-TIME!"

*Pantomime that you're honking a horn
several times with the fingers bent.*

---

example: Ieri sera in discoteca, ho conosciuto una
bionda mozzafiato che poi mi sono portato
a casa e... [do the gesture here].

translation: Last night at the dance club, I met a
breathtaking blond that I took home with
me and... [do the gesture here].

"I'M GONNA KICK YOUR ASS!"

(may be used figuratively or literally)

*Hold your hands in a position like you're holding
two guns with your index fingers pointing
downward, symbolizing a big butt.*

---

example 1: (used literally) Se non smetti di girare
intorno alla mia ragazza, ti faccio un culo
così!

translation: If you don't stop trying to pick up on my
girlfriend, I'm gonna kick your ass!

example 2: (used figuratively) Domani la Roma gioca
contro il Milan. Gli faremo un culo
incredibile!

translation: Tomorrow Rome is playing Milan. We're
gonna kick their ass big-time!

USED TO PREVENT BAD LUCK

*Touch your genitals with one hand and cover
the touching hand with your other hand.*

---

example: Quello è il nostro aereo. Guarda com'è
vecchio e scassato. Speriamo di arrivare.
Tocchiamoci le palle!

translation: That's our airplane. Look how old and
broken down it is. Let's hope we arrive
safely. Let's touch our genitals for good
luck!

THE "RASPBERRY"

Stick out your tongue and blow, making a farting sound.

---

example: Quando ho chiesto a Federico di prestarmi un po' di soldi, sai come mi ha risposto? Con una grossa pernacchia! [Do gesture here]

translation: When I asked Federico to lend me a little money, do you know how he answered me? With a big raspberry! [Do gesture here]

"BUTTON YOUR LIP!"

Pantomime sewing your mouth closed.

---

example: Fra un mese mi sposo. Non dire niente a nessuno. Acqua in bocca!

translation: In a month, I'm getting married. Don't say anything to anyone. Button your lip!

NOTE: **"Acqua in bocca!"** *exp.* "Button your lip!" • (lit.): "Water in mouth!"

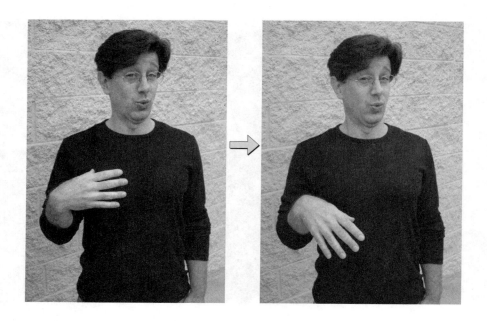

1. "WOW!" • 2. "HOW BORING!"

Fan yourself with one hand.

---

example 1: Voltati! Presto! Hai visto che minigonna? E che gambe! [Do gesture here]

translation: Turn around! Quick! Did you see that miniskirt? What legs! [Do gesture here]

example 2: Uffa! Che noia! [Do gesture here] Sono stufo di stare a sentire queste fesserie!

translation: Man! What a bore! [Do gesture here] I'm tired of listening to all this nonsense!

VARIATION: You can also use both hands in this gesture for extra emphasis.

LA LEGGE DELL'ELLE
(THE RULE OF THE "L")

Step 1: Make an "L" with your hand (which symbolizes a tall person with a small penis).

Step 2: Holding the "L," turn your hand so that your thumb is facing upward (which symbolizes a short person with a long penis).

---

example: Giovanni, sai, io sono più basso di te, però... [Do the gesture here]

translation: Giovanni, you know I may be shorter than you, but... [Do the gesture here]

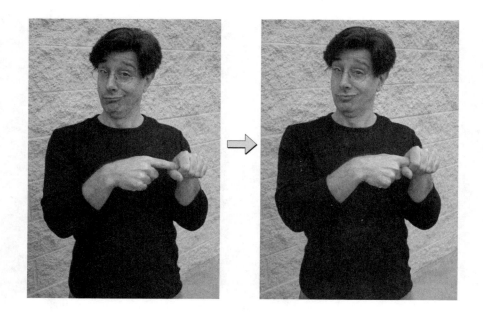

"I THINK THEY'RE HAVING SEX!"

Form a hole with one hand, and move the index finger
of your other hand in and out of the hole.

---

example: Vedi quei due là, dietro quel cespuglio? Mi
         sa che stiano... [Do gesture here]

translation: Do you see those two behind that bush?
             I think they're... [Do gesture here]

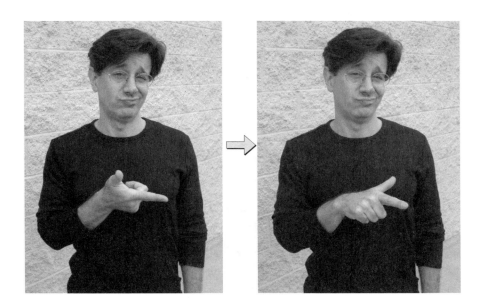

"THINGS DIDN'T WORK OUT"

Hold your finger like a gun and shake it back and forth.

---

example: Ieri sera ho portato fuori quella moretta carina che avevo conosciuto alla festa di Luca. Speravo di farci qualcosa, ma... [Do gesture here]

translation: Last night, I went out with that cute brunette that I met at Luke's party. I was hoping to "have some fun" with her, but... [Do gesture here]

"WHAT A GULLIBLE PERSON!"

Hook your mouth like you would a fish.

---

example: Ho appena detto a Simone che la mia famiglia è ricca sfondata, e lui ci ha abboccato come un pesce!

translation: I just told Simone that my family is ultra rich and he swallowed it hook, line, and sinker!

NOTE 1: **ricco sfondato/ricca sfondata** *exp.* extremely rich • (lit): bottomless rich.

NOTE 2: **abboccare come un pesce** *exp.* to believe everything one hears • (lit.): to eat the bait like a fish.

ANSWERS TO LESSONS 1-10

LEZIONE UNO – DATING SLANG

PRACTICE THE VOCABULARY

A. 1. bellone / bidone
    2. cazzoni
    3. galletto
    4. donnaioli / fisso

    5. fighetta / scopata
    6. metterti / mollano
    7. sporcaccioni / vista
    8. torno / pornazzo

B. 1. E
    2. C

    3. A
    4. F

    5. D
    6. B

C. 1. b
    2. a
    3. b

    4. a
    5. b
    6. a

    7. a
    8. b
    9. a

LEZIONE DUE – NONVULGAR INSULTS & PUTDOWNS

PRACTICE THE VOCABULARY

A. 1. C
    2. B
    3. D

    4. E
    5. A

B. 1. tappo
    2. becco
    3. leccapiedi / scatole
    4. frega

    5. spettegolare / pigrone
    6. noioso
    7. pelata / puzzolente
    8. morire / grande

C. 1. b   6. a   11. a
    2. b   7. b   12. b
    3. a   8. b   13. b
    4. a   9. a   14. a
    5. b   10. b   15. b

LEZIONE TRE – VULGAR INSULTS & NAME-CALLING

PRACTICE THE VOCABULARY

A. 1. D   4. A
    2. B   5. C
    3. E   6. F

B.

Giuseppe: Guarda quella *(whore)* __**bagascia**__!

Carmela: Che *(the hell)* __**diavolo**__ stai facendo? Che *(an asshole or "testicle")* __**coglione**__! Non sai guidare?

Alfredo: Maledetta *(prostitute)* __**puttana**__ ! Scommetto che *(she's on the rag)* __**ha le sue cose**__!

Carmela: *(Bastard)* __**Bastardo**__! Non sopporto i *(cocksuckers)* __**leccacazzi**__ come te! Va'a farti *(fucked)* __**fottere**__!

Giuseppe: Cacciatelo in *(ass)* __**culo**__!

Alfredo: Accidenti alla quella gran *(sow)* __**porca**__ di tua madre!

Giuseppe: Per poco non mi distrugge la macchina, e mi mostra il dito?! Va'al diavolo!

Carmela: *(Son of a bitch)* __**figlio di troia**__!

Giuseppe: *(Ass-licker)* __**leccaculi**__!

Alfredo: Giuseppe, lasciala perdere! Dobbiamo correre per non arrivare tardi in chiesa!

C. 1. a
    2. a
    3. b
    4. a
    5. b
    6. b
    7. b
    8. a
    9. a
    10. b
    11. b
    12. a
    13. b
    14. b

LEZIONE QUATTRO – SLANG SHOWING ANNOYANCE

PRACTICE THE VOCABULARY

A. 1. B
    2. D
    3. F
    4. A
    5. E
    6. C

B. 1. Muoio
    2. fesso
    3. schifoso / anima
    4. troiaio / rompiscatole
    5. fuori
    6. pelata / anni

C. 1. b
    2. a
    3. b
    4. b
    5. b
    6. a
    7. b
    8. b
    9. a

LEZIONE CINQUE – SEXUAL SLANG

PRACTICE THE VOCABULARY

A. 1. B
    2. F
    3. D
    4. G
    5. E
    6. A
    7. C

B.

Corrado: È una bellissima giornata! Che ne dici di fare due passi in centro?

Silvia: In centro? Ma è là dove c'è il quartiere a luci *(red)* __**rossi**__! È pieno di *(prostitutes)* __**puttane**__, *(pimps)* __**magnaccia**__ e *(whorehouses)* __**bordelli**__!

Corrado: Lo so, ma è interessante da vedere. Sai, l'ultima volta che sono passato da quelle parti, ho visto Fulvio con due troie. A dire il vero, ne stava baciando una con la lingua.

Silvia: Be', se gli piacciono, spero che almeno usi un *(rubber)* __**guanto**__. Sono certa che non vuole beccarsi l'AIDS.

Corrado: Immagino che voglia soltanto farsi fare un *(blowjob)* __**pompino**__, o magari fare una bella *(lay)* __**scopata**__. Soltanto l'idea di andare in un casino mi renderebbe così nervoso che non mi riuscirebbe nemmeno *(to get it up)* __**farlo rizzare**__!

C. 1. b   4. a   7. a
    2. a   5. b   8. b
    3. a   6. b   9. b

ANSWERS TO REVIEW EXAM 1-5

A. 1. a   7. b   13. b   19. a   25. b
    2. b   8. a   14. a   20. b   26. a
    3. b   9. a   15. a   21. b   27. b
    4. a   10. a   16. a   22. b   28. b
    5. a   11. b   17. a   23. b   29. b
    6. b   12. b   18. b   24. a

B. 1. bellone / bidone   5. spettegolare / pigrone
    2. donnaioli / fisso   6. schifoso / anima
    3. sporcaccioni / vista   7. pelata / anni
    4. torno / pornazzo

C. 1. D   4. A   7. B
    2. G   5. E   8. C
    3. F   6. H

LEZIONE SEI – BODILY FUNCTIONS AND SOUNDS

PRACTICE THE VOCABULARY

A. 1. B   3. E   5. C
    2. D   4. A   6. F

B.

Massimiliano: Prima che partiamo devo *(to take a leak)* __**fare un po' d'acqua**__ .

Edoardo: Sei sicuro? *(It stinks to high heaven)* __**Puzza da fare schifo**__ in quei *(shithouses)* __**cessi**__! Quel puzzo di *(shit)* __**merda**__ mi fa venir voglia di *(barf my guts up)* __**fare i gattini**__! C'è sempre un gran tanfo di *(the runs)* __**sciolta**__ là dentro! Abbastanza da farti diventare subito *(constipated)* __**stitico**__!

Massimiliano: Mi dispiace davvero dirtelo, ma credo che il tuo fratellino abbia appena *(farted)* __**fatto un peto**__ in pubblico, o che *(took a shit)* __**si sia cacato**__ nei pantaloni.

Edoardo: Nooo, Marchino! Di nuovo?

C. 1. b   4. b   7. a
    2. a   5. b   8. a
    3. a   6. b   9. a

LEZIONE SETTE – THE MANY USES OF "MERDA"

PRACTICE THE VOCABULARY

A. 1. C
    2. B
    3. D
    4. E
    5. A
    6. F

B.

Costanza: La sai l'ultima? Roberto era fuori con un'altra tipa, quando per caso ha incontrato la sua ragazza!

Antonella: (Shit) __**Merda**__ ! Roberto è il più gran (shithead) __**testone di merda**__ che abbia mai conosciuto! Ho sempre saputo che quella merda di Roberto prima o poi avrebbe (embarrassed) __**fatto una figure di merda**__ come quella. Sapevo anche che la sua storia con Angela sarebbe (to end miserably) __**finita in merda**__ un giorno o l'altro.

Costanza: Ho sempre saputo che era un (very despicable person) __**merdoso**__, ma mai fino a quel punto! Chi mai vorrebbe uscire con uno che è così (piece of shit) __**pezzo di merda**__? Non solo Roberto ha una gran (face) __**faccia**__ di merda, ma (he always stinks like shit) __**puzza sempre di merda**__ e la sua casa è un gran (dirty and disgusting place) __**merdaio**__!

Antonella: Sinceramente credo che la sua ragazza sia fortunata a mollare quello merdaiolo una volta per sempre!

C. 1. a   4. a   7. a
    2. a   5. b   8. a
    3. b   6. b   9. a

LEZIONE OTTO – THE MANY USES OF "CAGARE"

PRACTICE THE VOCABULARY

A. 1. F   3. E   5. C
     2. D   4. B   6. A

B.

Giorgio: Ieri notte sono stato scippato alla metro. Mi sono __**cagato**__ addosso dalla paura!

Filippo: Stai scherzando? Che è successo?

Giorgio: Beh, mi era venuta voglia di __**fare una cagata**__ e così mi ero messo a cercare un __**cacatoio**__. Quando sono entrato, c'era un altro tizio che __**cagava**__. Immagino che avesse la __**cacarella**__ o qualcosa di simile, perchè quel posto puzzava da morire! Comunque, mi sono infilato nel cesso accanto al suo. Quando sono uscito c'erano due omoni là fuori che aspettavano; sembravano tosti e dei gran __**cacasodo**__. Di solito io non sono un __**cacasotto**__, ma ho avuto subito l'impressione che ci sarebbero stati guai. All'improvviso, il più __**cacasenno**__ dei due, mi guarda in faccia e mi dice di dargli l'orologio. Beh, in quel momento non mi sono sentito in vena di fare nè il __**cacasentenze**__ nè il __**cacamiracoli**__ e così, gliel'ho dato. Oltre tutto il mio orologio non valeva un gran chè. Era una __**cagata**__ che comprai anni fa. Quando poi mi ha detto di allungargli tutti i miei soldi, gli ho risposto che non ne avevo. Allora lui mi ha mandato a __**cagare**__ e ha cominciato a rincorrermi!

Filippo: Mamma mia! Mi sarei cagato nei pantaloni anch'io!

C. 1. a   4. a   7. b
     2. b   5. b   8. a
     3. a   6. b   9. b

LEZIONE NOVE – THE MANY USES OF "CAZZO"

PRACTICE THE VOCABULARY

A. 1. D
    2. E
    3. A
    4. C
    5. B
    6. F

B.

Gabriele: Come vanno le cose con il tuo ospite?

Franco: Da fare schifo! Francesco non solo è una gran *(dickhead)*
    testa di cazzo, ma anche il più grande *(lazy bum)*
    fancazzista che abbia mai conosciuto. Non *(never
    does "dick" around the house)* **fa mai un cazzo** in casa.
    Non fa che guardare questi spettacoli televisivi *(shitty)*
    del cazzo tutto il giorno. Ma la cosa che *(pissed me off)*
    mi fa incazzare di più, sono tutte quelle *(bullshit)*
    cazzate che racconta. Ho l'impressione che si inventi
    tutto per far colpo sulla gente. *(How embarrassing)* **Che
    figura del cazzo!** La cosa peggiore poi, è che *(never minds
    his own business)* **non si fa mai i cazzi suoi**.

Gabriele: *(Damn)* **Cazzo!** È proprio un *(big idiot)* **cazzone**!

Franco: Fortunatamente se ne andrà fra un paio di giorni. Oh, no!
    È proprio lui e viene verso di noi! Chissà che *(the hell does he want)*
    cazzo vuole? Guarda come guida *(like an idiot)*
    alla cazzo! Sta guidando sul marciapiede! Spostati!

C. 1. a   4. b   7. b
    2. a   5. b   8. b
    3. a   6. a   9. a

LEZIONE DIECI – THE MANY USES OF "CULO"

PRACTICE THE VOCABULARY

A. 1. C   3. A   5. B
    2. E   4. D   6. F

B.

Federico: Arianna! *(What luck)* __**Che culo**__! Sono così contento di averti trovata. Non crederai a quello che è successo oggi. Conosci la proprietaria del negozio all'angolo?

Arianna: Vuoi dire quella *(fat ass)* __**culona**__ che lecca il *(ass)* __**culo**__ a tutti?

Federico: No, no! Non la *(butt-kisser)* __**leccaculo**__. Quella è la commessa. Parlo invece della proprietaria, quella con quel bel *(little butt)* __**culino**__ e quella terribile *(butt-ugly face)* __**faccia di culo**__. Bene, oggi ho visto un tipo che le gridava in faccia, perchè lei glielo ha *(cheated)* __**messo in culo**__ e ha cercato anche di farlo pagare! E lui continuava a gridare: "Questa è un'*(rip-off)* __**inculata**__!"

Arianna: Lo capisco, poveretto. Anch'io l'ho preso in culo da lei! Quella cerca sempre di aggiungere qualche lira alla tua carta di credito.

Federico: Bene, lei si è così arrabbiata con lui per averle gridato in faccia, che ha cominciato a *(make fun of him)* __**prenderlo per il culo**__. Alla fine poi gli ha anche detto *(fuck off)* __**vaffanculo**__! Ho davvero pensato che lei poi saltasse di là dal bancone e gli *(kick his ass)* __**facesse il culo**__!

C. 1. b.   5. b   9. b
    2. a   6. a   10. a
    3. b   7. a
    4. b   8. b

ANSWERS TO REVIEW EXAM 6-10

A. 1. a   7. a   13. b   19. b   25. b
    2. b   8. b   14. a   20. a   26. a
    3. a   9. a   15. a   21. b   27. b
    4. b   10. a   16. b   22. b   28. b
    5. a   11. b   17. a   23. a
    6. a   12. b   18. b   24. b

B. 1. che culo
    2. cazzo vuole / alla cazzo
    3. merda /testona di merda / fatto una figura di merda / finita in merda
    4. fare un po' d'acqua
    5. fatto un peto / si sia cacato

C. 1. C   4. E   7. A
    2. D   5. B   8. H
    3. G   6. F

D. 1. mani   5. giro   9. pizza
    2. lavandino 6. pasta   10. sfondato
    3. birra   7. colpi   11. flippata
    4. scatole   8. sbirro   12. chetarsi

APPENDIX

-DICTATIONS-

LEZIONE UNO

1. Massimo, il **bellone** che ho conosciuto la scorsa settimana, mi **ha tirato un bidone**!

2. Non faccio che conoscere dei gran **cazzoni** in giro.

3. A tutti piace **fare il galletto**.

4. Credo che siano tutti dei **donnaioli** e che tutti **abbiano quel chiodo fisso in testa**.

5. Ogni volta che vedono una bella **fighetta**, cercano di **beccarla** e danno per scontato che sia una **scopata facile**.

6. Non appena però pensano che tu voglia **metterti seriamente con loro**, loro ti **mollano**!

LEZIONE DUE

1. Ehi! C'è il nuovo impiegato, Roberto. Che **tappo**!

2. **Chiudi il becco**! Non lo sopporto!

3. È un **leccapiedi** da non crederci.

4. Tipi come lui mi **rompono davvero le scatole**.

5. E **non gliene frega**, niente del suo lavoro.

6. Passa gran parte del giorno a **spettegolare** al telefono con i suoi amici.

7. Quel tipo è un **pigrone**!

8. Non uscirei mai con un tipo **noioso** come quello!

LEZIONE TRE

1. Guarda quella **bagascia**!

2. **Che diavolo stai facendo**?

3. Che **coglione**! Non sai guidare?

4. **Maledetta puttana**! Scommetto che **ha le sue cose**.

5. **Bastardo**! Non sopporto i **leccacazzi** come te!

6. **Va'a farti fottere**!

7. **Cacciatelo in culo**!

8. **Accidenti alla quella gran porca di tua madre**!

LEZIONE QUATTRO

1. Mamma mia! **Muoio dalla noia** qui!

2. Il marito di Ornella è così **fesso**!

3. È sempre un **guastafeste**!

4. È così **schifoso**! Pensavo addirittura di **vomitare l'anima**!

5. E poi la loro casa è **un troiaio**!

6. Che **rompiscatole** è lei! E suo marito è quel **grassone** là.

7. Credo anche che sia **un po'di fuori**.

8. A dire il vero **porta davvero male gli anni**.

LEZIONE CINQUE

1. Ma è là dove c'è il **quartiere a luci rosse**!

2. È pieno di **puttane**, **magnaccia** e **bordelli**!

3. Sai, l'ultima volta che sono passato da quelle parti, ho visto Fulvio con due **troie**.

4. A dire il vero, ne stava **baciando una con la lingua**.

5. Be', se gli piacciono, spero che almeno usi un **guanto**.

6. Sono certa che non vuole beccarsi **l'AIDS**.

7. Immagino che voglia soltanto farsi fare un **pompino**, o magari fare una **bella scopata**.

8. Soltanto l'idea di andare in un **casino** mi renderebbe così nervoso che non mi riuscirebbe nemmeno **farlo rizzare**!

LEZIONE SEI

1. Prima che partiamo devo **fare un po' d'acqua**.

2. **Puzza da fare schifo** in quei **cessi**!

3. Quel puzzo di **merda** mi fa venir voglia di **fare i gattini**!

4. C'è sempre un gran tanfo di **sciolta** là dentro.

5. Abbastanza da farti diventare subito **stitico**.

6. Mi dispiace davvero dirtelo, ma credo che il tuo fratellino abbia appena **fatto un peto** in pubblico, o che **si sia cacato** nei pantaloni.

LEZIONE SETTE

1. **Merda**! Roberto è il più gran **testone di merda** che abbia mai conosciuto!

2. Ho sempre saputo che quella **merda** di Roberto prima o poi avrebbe **fatto una figura di merda** come quella.

3. Sapevo anche che la sua storia con Angela sarebbe **finita in merda** un giorno o l'altro.

4. Ho sempre saputo che era un **merdoso**, ma mai fino a quel punto!

5. Chi mai vorrebbe uscire con uno che è così **pezzo di merda**?

6. Non solo Roberto ha una gran **faccia di merda**, ma **puzza sempre di merda** e la sua casa è un gran **merdaio**!

LEZIONE OTTO

1. Ieri notte sono stato scippato alla metro. Mi **sono cagato addosso dalla paura**!

2. Beh, mi era venuta voglia di **fare una cagata** e così mi ero messo a cercare un **cacatoio**.

3. Quando sono entrato, c'era un altro tizio che **cagava**.

4. Immagino che avesse **la cacarella**, o qualcosa di simile, perchè quel posto puzzava da morire!

5. Di solito io non sono un **cacasotto**, ma ho avuto subito l'impressione che ci sarebbero stati guai.

6. All'improvviso, il più **cacasenno** dei due, mi guarda in faccia e mi dice di dargli l'orologio.

7. Beh, in quel momento non mi sono sentito in vena di fare nè il **cacasentenze** nè il **cacamiracoli** e così, gliel'ho dato.

8. Era una **cagata** che comprai anni fa.

LEZIONE NOVE

1. Francesco non solo è una gran **testa di cazzo**, ma anche il più grande **fancazzista** che abbia mai conosciuto.

2. Non **fa mai un cazzo** in casa.

3. Non fa che guardare questi spettacoli televisivi **del cazzo** tutto il giorno.

4. Ma la cosa che **mi fa incazzare** di più, sono tutte quelle **cazzate** che racconta.

5. **Che figura del cazzo**! La cosa peggiore poi, è che **non si fa mai i cazzi suoi**.

6. **Cazzo**! È proprio un **cazzone**!

7. È proprio lui e viene verso di noi! Chissà che **cazzo vuole**?

8. Guarda come guida **alla cazzo**!

LEZIONE DIECI

1. **Che culo**!

2. Vuoi dire quella **culona** che **lecca il culo a tutti**?

3. Questa è un'**inculata**!

4. Anch'io l'ho **preso in culo** da lei!

5. Alla fine poi gli ha anche detto **vaffanculo**!

6. Ho davvero pensato che lei poi saltasse di là dal bancone e gli **facesse il culo**!

GLOSSARY

"Accidenti a quella gran porca di tua madre!" *interj.*
"Screw you!" • (lit.): "Damn that big sow of your mother!"

example:
Oh, stupido bastardo! Ma devi imparare a guidare! **Accidenti a quella gran porca di tua madre**!

translation:
Oh, you stupid bastard! You need to learn how to drive! **Screw you**!

SYNONYM 1:
"Accidenti a quella gran maiala di tua madre!" *interj.* • (lit.): "Damn that big sow of your mother!"

SYNONYM 2:
"Accidenti a quella gran puttana di tua madre!" *interj.* • (lit.): "Damn that big whore of your mother!"

SYNONYM 3:
"Accidenti a quella gran troia di tua madre!" *interj.* • (lit.): "Damn that big sow of your mother!"

AIDS *m.* AIDS (an abbreviation for "Sindrome da immunodeficienza acquisita").

example:
Massimo continua ad andare a puttane senza preservativo! Uno di questi giorni si beccherà l'**AIDS**.

translation:
Massimo keeps going to prostitutes without using a condom! One of these days he's going to catch **AIDS**.

NOTE:
It's interesting to note that in Italian, the abbreviation for

Sindrome da immunodeficienza acquisita (AIDS) is backward and not SDIA as one would think!

---

alito puzzolente *m.* bad breath • (lit.): stinking breath.

example:
Matteo ha un **alito** così **puzzolente** che lo sento anche al telefono! Davvero non invidio la sua ragazza!

translation:
Matteo's got such a **bad breath** that I can even smell it over the phone! I really don't envy his girlfriend!

SYNONYM:
alito fetente *m.* • (lit.): stinking breath.

---

alla cazzo *adv.* said of something done in an idiotic way • (lit.): in the manner of the dick, dick-like.

example:
Quella vecchietta guida proprio **alla cazzo**! Se non fa attenzione andrà a battere contro quel palo!

translation:
That little old lady drives **like a jerk**! If she doesn't pay attention, she's going to hit that pole!

VARIATION:
alla cazzo di cane *adv.* • (lit.): in the manner of a dog's dick.

SYNONYM:
alla boia *adv.* • (lit.): in the manner of the executioner.

allocco *m.* a stupid person, a jerk • (lit.): owl.

example:
Cosimo è davvero un **allocco**! Lo hanno preso in giro tutta la sera e lui ha creduto a tutto quello che gli hanno raccontato!

translation:
Cosimo is such a **dolt**! They have been teasing him all night and he believed everything he was told!

SYNONYM 1:
bischero *m.* (Tuscany).

SYNONYM 2:
coglione *m.* • (lit.): testicle.

SYNONYM 3:
credulone *m.*

SYNONYM 4:
cretino *m.* • (lit.): cretin.

SYNONYM 5:
fava *m.* • (lit.): fava bean.

SYNONYM 6:
fesso *m.* • (lit.): from the feminine noun *fessura* meaning "crack" as in "a crack in one's head."

SYNONYM 7:
imbecille *m.* • (lit.): imbecile.

SYNONYM 8:
oca *f.* • (lit.): goose, referring to a female "dolt."

SYNONYM 9:
scemo/a *n.* • (from the verb *scemare*, meaning "to shrink or diminish").

amore a prima vista *exp.* love at first sight.

example:
Lorenzo e Cecilia si sono incontrati recentemente ad una festa di Carnevale. Si sono parlati per alcuni minuti e si sono scambiati i loro numeri di telefono. È stato **amore a prima vista**!

translation:
Lorenzo and Cecilia met recently at a carnival party. They talked for a few minutes and exchanged phone numbers. It was **love at first sight**!

SYNONYM:
un colpo di fulmine *exp.* • (lit.): a thunderbolt (of love).

---

avere le proprie cose *exp.* to be on the rag, to menstruate • (lit.): to have one own things.

example:
Mamma mia! È impossibile parlare con Giulia oggi! Deve **avere le sue cose**!

translation:
Geez! It's impossible to talk to Giulia today! She must **be on the rag**!

SYNONYM 1:
avere il marchese *exp.* (more vulgar) • (lit.): to have the marquise.

SYNONYM 2:
avere le mestruazioni *exp.* • (lit.): to menstruate.

avere un chiodo fisso in testa *exp.* to be fixated on something • (lit.): to have a nail fixed in the head.

example:
Giorgio pensa ad Elena giorno e notte. Lui ha davvero un **chiodo fisso in testa**.

translation:
Giorgio thinks about Elena day and night. He's truly **fixated on her**.

---

baciare con la lingua *exp.* to French kiss • (lit.): to kiss with the tongue.

example:
Sabato scorso Francesco è uscito con una sua compagna di classe e l'ha **baciata con la lingua** davanti al cinema.

translation:
Last Saturday, Francesco went out with one of his classmates and **French kissed** her in front of the movie theater.

SYNONYM 1:
pomiciare *v.* • (lit.): to pumice (from *pomice*, meaning "pumice stone" which is used by rubbing it against something else).

SYNONYM 2:
slinguare *v.* • (lit.): to "tongue" (from the feminine noun *lingua*, meaning "tongue."

bagascia *f.* whore, slut.

example:
Marina è davvero una gran **bagascia**. Alle feste si fa toccare da tutti i ragazzi!

translation:
Marina is really a **slut**. She lets all the guys touch her at the parties!

SYNONYM 1:
cagna *f.* female dog, bitch.

SYNONYM 2:
maiala *f.* • (lit.): sow, female pig.

SYNONYM 3:
puttana *f.* • (lit.): prostitute.

SYNONYM 4:
vacca *f.* • (lit.): cow.

ALSO:
figlio/a di troia *m.* son/daughter of a bitch • (lit.): son/daughter of a sow.

---

bastardo/a *n.* • (lit.): bastard.

example:
Enrico è un **bastardo** fetente! Ieri ha telefonato alla mia ragazza e le ha chiesto di uscire!

translation:
Enrico is a stinking **bastard**! Yesterday he called my girlfriend and asked her out!

SYNONYM 1:
figlio di puttana *m.* • (lit.): son of a whore.

SYNONYM 2:
stronzo/a *n.* • (lit.): turd.

beccare qualcuno *v.* to hit on someone, to pick someone up • (lit.): to peck.

example:
Ieri sera sono andato in un locale e ho **beccato** un' incredibile ragazza scandinava che sedeva al tavolo accanto al mio.

translation:
Last night, I went to a bar and **picked up** an incredible Scandinavian girl who sat at the table next to mine.

NOTE:
locale *m.* club or night club.

---

bella scopata (una) *f.* a good lay, a good "boink" • (lit.): a good fuck.

example:
Ieri sera Massimiliano è uscito con Patrizia; sono andati al cinema e poi hanno fatto **una bella scopata** sulla spiaggia.

translation:
Last night, Massimiliano went out with Patrizia. They went to the movies and then had **a good boink** at the beach.

SYNONYM 1:
bombata *f.* • (lit.): from the feminine noun *bomba*, meaning "bomb."

SYNONYM 2:
chiavata *f.* • (lit.): from the feminine noun *chiave*, meaning "key," suggesting that the person can be easily "opened."

SYNONYM 3:
ciulata f. (Northern Italy).

SYNONYM 4:
pigiata f. • (lit.): from the verb *pigiare*, meaning "to push," suggesting that the person can be easily pushed into.

ALSO 1:
cosina veloce (una) f. a quickie • (lit.): a quick little thing.

ALSO 2:
sveltina (una) f. a quickie • (lit.): from the adjective *svelto/a*, meaning "quick."

---

bellone m. a hunk, a man who is very good-looking yet stuck up.

example:
Ieri sera sono stata ad una festa con dei miei amici e ho conosciuto un gran **bellone** che si chiama Alessandro.

translation:
Last night, I went to a party with some friends and met a big **hunk** named Alessandro.

NOTE:
This comes from the masculine noun *fico*, meaning "a good-looking, attractive, and well built young man who wears trendy clothes."

SYNONYM 1:
fichetto n.

SYNONYM 2:
figo della Madonna exp.

SYNONYM 3:
figone n.

bordello m. • **1.** brothel, whorehouse • **2.** big mess.

example 1:
Tutti nel quartiere sono molto scontenti perchè hanno appena aperto un **bordello** vicino alla scuola!

translation:
The neighborhood is very upset because a **brothel** just opened next to the school!

example 2:
Raffaello non pulisce mai il suo appartamento. Non hai idea di come è dentro. Che **bordello**!

translation:
Raffaello never cleans his apartment. You wouldn't believe what it looks like inside. What a **mess**!

SYNONYM 1:
casa chiusa f. • (lit.): closed house.

SYNONYM 2:
casa di malaffare f. • (lit.): house of bad/dirty business.

SYNONYM 3:
casa di tolleranza f. • (lit.): house of tolerance.

SYNONYM 4:
casino m.

SYNONYM 5:
lupanare m. (from the Latin word *lupa*, meaning "she wolf," which is slang for "prostitute").

SYNONYM 6:
postribolo m.

NOTE:
Brothels are currently illegal in Italy. They were all shut down in the late 50s.

cacamiracoli (un/una) *n.*
someone who takes a lot of time, makes a lot of difficulties before giving up/granting something, a stingy person • (lit.): one who shits miracles.

example:
Roberto è un gran **cacamiracoli**! Tutte le volte che lo prego di prestarmi la sua macchina per un paio d'ore, fa un sacco di storie!

translation:
Roberto is a very **stingy person**! Everytime I ask him to lend me his car for a couple of hours, he makes such a fuss!

cacarella *f.* • (lit.): the shits (from the verb *cacare*, meaning "to shit").
example:
Dopo aver mangiato della carne schifosa, ieri, ho avuto la **cacarella** per tre giorni!

translation:
After eating some bad meat yesterday, I had **the runs** for three days!

cacarsi nei pantaloni *exp.*
to be scared shitless • (lit.): to shit in one's pants.

example:
Quando ho visto che quella macchina che accelerava verso di me, **mi sono cacato nei pantaloni**.

translation:
When I saw that car speeding toward me, **I was scared shitless**.

cacasenno (un/una) *n.* a
know-it-all, a smart-ass • (lit.): one who shits wisdom.

example:
Giulio è proprio un **cacasenno**! Crede di sapere tutto, ma in realtà non sa un cazzo!

translation:
Giulio is really a **smart-ass**! He thinks he knows everything, but he actually doesn't know shit!

SYNONYM 1:
cacasentenze (un/una) *n.* • (lit.): moral shitter.

SYNONYM 2:
saccente (un/una) *n.* • (lit.): from the verb *sapere*, meaning "to know."

SYNONYM 3:
saputo un/una saputa *n.* • (lit.): from the verb *sapere*, meaning "to know."

SYNONYM 4:
sputasentenze (un/una) *n.* • (lit.): moral spitter.

cacasentenze (un/una) n.
one who likes to moralize; one who acts like he/she is very smart, a smart-ass • (lit.): one who shits sentences.

example:
Marco è un **cacasentenze** con tutti; anche con i suoi genitori! In realtà però non credo che abbia idea di quello che dice!

translation:
Marco is a **smart-ass** with everybody, even with his parents! But I truly don't think he has a clue about what he's saying!

cacasodo (un/una) n.
an arrogant person, someone who thinks his/her shit doesn't stink • (lit.): one who takes a hard shit (from the verb *cacare*, meaning "to shit" and the adjective *sodo/a*, meaning "tough" or "hard").

example:
Quel buttafuori è un gran **cacasodo**. Si comporta come se fosse il padrone del locale.

translation:
That bouncer **thinks his shit doesn't shink**. He acts as if he were the owner of the club.

cacasotto (un/una) n.
a very fearful person, a "chicken-shit" • (lit): one who shits down below.

example:
Serena è davvero una **cacasotto**! Non ha mai il coraggio di entrare in quel vecchio cimitero abbandonato, di notte.

translation:
Serena is really a **chicken-shit**! She never has the guts to walk into that old abandoned cemetery at night.

cacatoio m.
(very vulgar) the "shithouse," the "crapper," a place where one takes a shit • (lit.): shitter (from the verb *cacare*, meaning "to shit").

example:
Se non trovo subito un **cacatoio** pubblico, mi cagherò addosso!

translation:
If I don't find a **crapper** immediately, I'm going to shit in my pants!

SYNONYM:
cesso m.

"Cacciatelo in culo!" interj.
"Up yours!" • (lit): "Stick it in your ass!"

example:
Figlio di puttana, **cacciatelo in culo**!

translation:
You son of a bitch, **stick it up your ass**!

cagare/cacare *v.* to defecate •
(lit.): to shit.

example:
Giuseppe deve aver appena
cagato. Nel bagno non si respira!

translation:
Giuseppe must have just **taken a
shit**. You can't breathe in the
bathroom!

SYNONYM:
See – **fare una cagata/cacata**,
p. 112, 208.

ALSO:
andare a cagare *interj.* to fuck
off • (lit): to go shit • *Va'a cagare!;*
Fuck off!/Fuck you!

**cagarsi/cacarsi addosso
dalla paura** *exp.* to be scared
shitless • (lit.): to shit on oneself for
fear.

example:
Quando ho visto la polizia che
sparava a pochi metri da me, **mi
sono cagato/cacato addosso
dalla paura**!

translation:
When I saw the police shooting a
few feet from where I was standing,
I **was scared shitless**!

SYNONYM 1:
farsela sotto dalla paura *exp.*
• (lit.): to make it down below on
oneself for fear.

SYNONYM 2:
**pisciarsi addosso dalla
paura** *exp.* • (lit.): to pee on
oneself for fear.

**cagarsi/cacarsi nei
pantaloni** *exp.* to be scared
shitless • (lit.): to shit in one's
pants.

example:
Quando il rapinatore mi ha
puntato la pistola in faccia, **mi
sono cagato nei pantaloni**!

translation:
When the robber pointed the
gun in my face, I **was shitting
in my pants**!

SYNONYM:
farsela nei pantaloni *exp.* •
(lit.): to do it in one's pants.

cagata/cacata (una) *f.*
bullshit, something worthless, a
piece of shit • (lit.): a shit.

example:
Quest'orologio che ho comprato
l'anno scorso per due soldi, è
proprio una **cagata**!

translation:
This watch I bought last year for
a few bucks is really a **piece of
crap**!

SYNONYM 1:
boiata (una) *f.* • (lit.): from
the masculine noun *boia*,
meaning "executer."

SYNONYM 2:
cazzata (una) *f.* • (lit.): from
the masculine noun *cazzo*,
meaning "penis" or "dick."

SYNONYM 3:
cretinata (una) *f.* • (lit.): from the adjective *cretino/a,* meaning "cretin."

SYNONYM 4:
fesseria (una) *f.* • (lit.): from the masculine noun *fesso,* meaning "crack."

SYNONYM 5:
merdata (una) *f.* • (lit.): from the feminine noun *merda,* meaning "shit."

SYNONYM 6:
puttanata (una) *f.* • (lit.): from the feminine noun *puttana,* meaning "whore."

SYNONYM 7:
stronzata (una) *f.* • (lit.): from the mascuine noun *stronzo,* meaning "turd."

SYNONYM 8:
stupidaggine (una) *f.* • (lit.): from the adjective *stupido/a,* meaning "stupid."

---

casino *m.* • **1.** brothel, a whore-house • **2.** a big mess • **3.** an incredible loud noise.

example 1:
L'anno scorso, quando Graziano è andato in Asia, è stato anche in un **casino** di Bangkok, dove tutte le puttane avevano meno di vent' anni.

translation:
Last year, when Graziano went to Asia, he also went to a **brothel** in Bangkok, where all the girls were under twenty.

example 2:
Questa stanza è un gran **casino**! Ci sono carte e vestiti dappertutto!

translation:
This room is a big mess! There are papers and clothes everywhere!

example 3:
Ieri sera, al concerto dei Backstreet Boys, tutti ballavano e gridavano; c'era un **casino** incredibile!

translation:
Last night at the Backstreet Boys concert, everyone danced and screamed; it was incredibly **noisy**!

SYNONYMS:
See – **bordello**, *p. 68, 195.*

---

cazzata (una) *f.* • **1.** bullshit • **2.** something worthless, a piece of shit.

example 1:
Quello che dici è una **cazzata**! Non è vero che Carlotta ed io usciamo insieme.

translation:
What you're saying is **bullshit**! It's not true that Carlotta and I are going out together.

example 2:
Questo bell'orologio che ho comprato ieri si è già fermato! Che **cazzata**!

translation:
This beautiful watch I bought yesterday already stopped! What a **piece of shit**!

SYNONYM 1:
bischerata (una) f. (Tuscan) • (lit.): from the masculine noun *bischero*, meaning "penis."

SYNONYM 2:
cavolata (una) f. • (lit.): from the masculine noun *cavolo*, meaning "cabbage."

SYNONYM 3:
cosa da niente (una) f. • (lit.): a thing of nothing.

SYNONYM 4:
fesseria (una) f. • (lit.): from the noun *fesso*, meaning "crack."

SYNONYM 5:
puttanata (una) f. • (lit.): from the feminine noun *puttana*, meaning "whore."

SYNONYM 6:
scemata (una) f. • (lit.): from the verb *scemare*, meaning "to shrink."

"Cazzo!" *interj.* "Damn!" or "Shit!" • (lit.): "Dick!"

example:
Cazzo! Se non mi muovo, perdo l'autobus!

translation:
Damn! If I don't get moving, I'm going to miss the bus!

SYNONYM 1:
"Figa!" *interj.* (an extremely vulgar term for "vagina") "Pussy!"

SYNONYM 2:
"Merda!" *interj.* • (lit.): "Shit!"

---

cazzo (del) *adv.* worthless, of bad quality, shitty (when used to modify a noun) • (lit.): of the dick.

example:
È stato proprio un concerto **del cazzo**! Le canzoni erano bruttissime e non cantavano nemmeno dal vivo!

translation:
It truly was a **shitty** concert! The songs were really bad and they didn't even play live!

---

cazzo (un) *m.* nothing, zip • (lit.): a dick.

example 1:
–C'è qualcosa da mangiare stasera?
–No, **non c'è un cazzo** in frigo!

translation:
–Is there anything to eat tonight?
–No, **there's shit** in the refrigerator!

example 2:
Gino **non sa un cazzo** di macchine!

translation:
Gino **doesn't know shit** about cars!

SYNONYM 1:
accidente (un) *m.* • (lit.): an accident.

SYNONYM 2:
bel niente (un) m. • (lit.): a beautiful nothing.

SYNONYM 3:
mazza (una) f. (very vulgar) • (lit.): a stick.

SYNONYM 4:
sega (una) f. (very vulgar) • (lit.): a saw.

---

cazzone m. jerk, ass hole • (lit.): big "dick."

example:
Il tipo che ho conosciuto alla cena di Giovanni era un gran **cazzone**! Ha cercato di abbracciare e baciare tutte le ragazze carine che erano lì.

translation:
The guy I met at Giovanni's dinner party was a real **jerk**! He tried to hug and kiss all the cute girls who were there.

SYNONYM:
stronzo n. • (lit.): turd.

---

cazzone/a n. a very stupid person, a "dickhead" • (lit.): a big dick.

example:
Alberto è proprio un **cazzone**. Non capisce mai le barzellette che gli raccontiamo. Dobbiamo sempre spiegargliele.

translation:
Alberto is a real **dickhead**. He never get the jokes we tell him. We always have to explain them to him.

SYNONYMS:
See – **fesso/a**, p. 55, 209.

---

cesso m. (vulgar) public bathroom, "shithouse."

example:
Devo andare in bagno! C'è un **cesso** qui vicino?

translation:
I need to go to the bathroom. Is there a **shithouse** near here?

SYNONYM 1:
cacatoio m.

SYNONYM 2:
pisciatoio m. • (lit.): a pisser (from the verb *pisciare*, meaning "to piss").

"Che cazzo vuole?" exp. "What the fuck does he/she want?" • (lit.): "What dick does he/she want?"

example:
Che cazzo vuole? Perchè non smette di suonarmi? Non vede che sta guidando contro mano?

translation:
What the hell does he want? Why doesn't he stop honking at me? Doesn't he realize that he's driving the wrong way?

SYNONYM:
"Che cavolo vuole?" exp. (euphemism) • (lit.): "What cabbage does he/she want?"

"Che culo!" *interj.* "What luck!" • (lit.): "What an ass!"

example:
Che culo! Stefania ha vinto alla lotteria!

translation:
What luck! Stefania won the lottery!

NOTE:
This interjection is somewhat vulgar, yet extremely common among younger people.

SYNONYM 1:
"Che mele!" *interj.* • (lit.): "What apples!"

NOTE:
Mele, literally "apples," is slang for one's rear end.

SYNONYM 2:
"Che paiolo!" *interj.* • (lit.): "What a copper pot!"

NOTE:
Paiolo, literally "a copper pot," is slang for one's rear end.

Che diavolo stai facendo?
exp. What the hell are you doing? • (lit.): What the devil are you doing?

example:
Mario, **che diavolo stai facendo**? Lasciala stare. Non vedi che Monica è venuta alla festa con il suo ragazzo?

translation:
Mario, **what the hell are you doing**? Leave her alone. Don't you see that Monica has come to the party with her boyfriend?

SYNONYM:
Che cazzo stai facendo?
exp. (more vulgar) What the fuck are you doing? • (lit.): What dick are you doing?

"Che figura del cazzo!"
interj. "How embarrassing!" • (lit.): "What a figure of the dick!"

example:
Mario è tornato a casa ieri sera e sua moglie ha subito notato che aveva dei signi di rossetto sul collo e sulla bocca! **Che figura del cazzo**!

translation:
Mario got back home last night and right away his wife noticed some lipstick marks on his neck and mouth! **How embarrassing**!

SYNONYM:
"Che figura di merda!"
interj. • (lit.): "What a figure of shit!"

---

chiudere il becco *exp.* to shut up, to shut one's trap • (lit.): to close the beak.

example:
Quando quella grassona ha cominciato ad offenderlo in pubblico, Luigi le ha detto di **chiudere il becco** e di levarsi di torno.

translation:
When that fat lady started to offend him in public, Luigi told her to **shut her trap** and get out of his way.

SYNONYM 1:
chetarsi v. • (lit.): to silence oneself.

SYNONYM 2:
stare zitto/a exp. • (lit.): to stay silent.

---

coglione m. asshole, jerk, idiot • (lit.): testicle.

example:
Giovanni è così **coglione**. Mi ha rotto lui la bici, e ha dato la colpa a qualcun altro.

translation:
Giovanni is such a **jerk**. He broke my bike and blamed it on someone else.

SYNONYM 1:
cazzone m. • (lit.): big dick.

SYNONYM 2:
fava f. • (lit.): fava bean, but also the head of the dick in Tuscan slang.

SYNONYM 3:
fesso m. • (lit.): from the feminine noun fessura meaning "crack" as in "a crack in one's head."

SYNONYM 4:
imbecille m. • (lit.): imbecile.

SYNONYM 5:
scemo/a n. • (from the verb scemare, meaning "to shrink" or "to diminish").

culino m. a small ass (from the masculine noun culo, meaning "ass").

example:
Sara ha proprio un bel **culino**! E guarda come lo muove!

translation:
Sara really has a cute **little butt**! And look how she moves it!

SYNONYM 1:
culetto m. • (lit.): little buttocks.

SYNONYM 2:
meline m. • (lit.): small apples (from the feminine noun mela, meaning "apple").

SYNONYM 3:
sederino m. • (lit.): "sitter" (from the verb sedere, meaning "to sit").

---

culone/a n. one with a big, fat ass (from the masculine noun culo, meaning "ass").

example:
Quella **culona** di Federica vuole uscire con me, ma io non voglio nemmeno pensarci!

translation:
That **fat ass** Federica wants to go out with me, but I don't even want to think about it!

di merda *adv.* lousy, shitty • (lit.): of shit.

example:

Ieri sera siamo stati ad una festa **di merda**! C'erano pochissime ragazze e quelle che erano lì erano bruttissime; il cibo e la musica poi erano terribili!

translation:

Last night, we went to a **shitty** party! There were only a few girls, and the ones who were there were actually very ugly. The food and the music then were just terrible!

SYNONYM:
del cazzo *adv.* • (lit.): of the dick.

donnaiolo *m.* womanizer, someone who chases women, a playboy.

example:

Enrico non fa altro che guardare le ragazze! Che **donnaiolo**! Ieri sera, al locale, ha offerto da bere a tutte le ragazze che ha conosciuto!

translation:

Enrico does nothing but look at girls! What a **playboy**! Last night at the club, he bought drinks for all the girls he met!

NOTE:
This comes from *donna*, meaning "woman."

essere un po'di fuori *exp.* to a little wacky, to be out of one's mind • (lit.): to be a little bit out.

example:

Quella vecchia donna è **un po'di fuori**. Continua a parlare con tutti quei turisti e non sa nemmeno cosa dice.

translation:

That old woman is **a little wacky**. She keeps talking to all those tourists and doesn't even know what she's saying.

SYNONYM 1:
essere fuori di testa *exp.* • (lit.): to be outside of head.

SYNONYM 2:
non esserci con la testa *exp.* • (lit.): not to be there with the head.

faccia di culo *f.* • **1.** a butt-ugly face • **2.** used as an insult, referring to a big jerk (lit.): face of ass.

example 1:

Matteo ha proprio una **faccia di culo**! Non so come farà a trovar moglie!

translation:

Matteo really has a **butt-ugly face**! I wonder how he'll get married!

example 2:

Fermati, **faccia di culo**! Non vedi che il semaforo è rosso?

translation:

Stop, **you fucking idiot**! Don't you see that the light is red?

SYNONYM 1:

faccia di cazzo f. • (lit.): dickface.

SYNONYM 2:

faccia di merda f. • (lit.): shitface.

---

faccia di merda f. a very despicable person, an asshole, a bastard, a son of a bitch • (lit.): a face of shit.

example:

Augusto ha proprio una gran **faccia di merda**! Tutte le volte che vede la mia ragazza, fa qualche commento stronzo sui suoi vestiti.

translation:

Augusto is really a **bastard**! Every single time he sees my girlfriend, he's got some nasty comment to make about her clothes.

SYNONYM 1:

faccia di cazzo f. • (lit.): dick face.

SYNONYM 2:

faccia di ciola f.

SYNONYM 3:

faccia di stronzo f. • (lit.): turd head.

---

fancazzista n. a lazy bum, a "lazy sack of shit" • (lit.): dick doer (from the expression *fare un cazzo*, literally meaning "to do a dick").

example:

Armando è un gran **fancazzista**! Lo hanno assunto la settimana scorsa e sta tutto il giorno a scrivere messaggi elettronici ai suoi amici.

translation:

Armando is a **lazy sack of shit**. They hired him last week and he spends the whole day writing email to his friends!

SYNONYM 1:

fannullone/a n. • (lit.): do-nothing (from *fare nulla*, meaning "to do nothing.")

SYNONYM 2:

pigrone/a n. • (lit.): a big lazy bum.

---

fare i gattini exp. to barf, to vomit • (lit.): to make the kittens.

example:

Chiara ha mangiato qualcosa al ristorante che era andato a male e quando è tornata a casa ha **fatto i gattini**.

translation:
Chiara ate something at the restaurant that had turned bad and when she went back home, she **threw up**.

---

fare il culo a qualcuno *exp.* to kick somebody's ass • (lit.): to make the ass to somebody.

example:
Ehi, tu! Se non lasci stare la mia ragazza, vengo lì e ti **faccio il culo**!

translation:
Hey, you! If you don't leave my girlfriend alone, I'm going to come over there and **kick your butt**!

SYNONYM:
fare la festa a qualcuno *exp.* • (lit.): to do the party to somebody.

ALSO:
farsi il culo *exp.* to work hard towards a goal, to work one's butt off • (lit.): to do one's butt • *Mi sono fatto il culo per quasi due mesi a studiare, e ho superato l'esame brillantemente!;* I worked my butt off studying for two months and passed the exam with flying colors!

NOTE:
A common Italian expression using both *fare il culo* and *farsi il culo* is: *O ti fai il culo, o te la fanno!;* You either work your butt off or they will kick your butt!

---

fare il galletto *exp.* to flirt • (lit.): to do like the rooster.

example:
Sabato sera, in discoteca, un ragazzo italiano ha **fatto il galletto** con me tutta la sera.

translation:
Saturday night at the dance club, an Italian guy **flirted** with me all night.

SYNONYM 1: **flirtare** *v.* (from English).

SYNONYM 2:
provarci *v.* (lit.): to give it a try.

---

fare il grande *exp.* to show off, to act like someone big • (lit.): to do the big.

example:
Tutte le estati, al mare, Raffaele **fa il grande** con tutte le ragazze nuove. Prima le porta in giro con la sua nuova macchina, poi offre a tutte bibite e gelati!

translation:
Every summer at the beach, Raffaele **shows off** with all the new girls. First of all, he takes them for a ride in his new car, then buys drinks and ice cream for everybody!

---

fare impazzire qualcuno *exp.* to drive someone crazy • (lit.): to make someone crazy.

example:
Massimiliano a volte è che così insistente che **mi fa impazzire**. Gli ho già detto un milione di volte che non mi interessa uscire con lui!

translation:
Sometimes Massimiliano is so persistent that **he drives me crazy**. I have already told him a million times that I'm not interested in going out with him.

SYNONYM:
mandare qualcuno fuori di cervello exp. • (lit.): to send someone out of his/her brain.

---

fare incazzare qualcuno
exp. to piss someone off.

example:
Gianna **mi fa sempre incazzare**. Tutte le volte che le chiedo se vuol mettersi con me, mi dice che non è pronta.

translation:
Gianna **always pisses me off**. Every time I ask her if she wants to be my girlfriend, she answers that she's not ready.

SYNONYM 1:
fare arrabbiare qualcuno exp.

SYNONYM 2:
fare incavolare qualcuno exp. (euphemism) • (lit.): to turn someone into cabbage.

SYNONYM 3:
mandare qualcuno in bestia exp. • (lit.): to send someone to the beast.

fare un peto exp. to fart • (lit.): to make a fart.

example:
Dopo aver mangiato tutti quei fagioli, **farai peti** a ripetizione!

translation:
After eating all those beans, you're going **to fart** nonstop!

SYNONYM 1:
cureggiare v.

SYNONYM 2:
fare aria exp. • (lit.): to make air.

SYNONYM 3:
fare una cureggia exp.

SYNONYM 4:
fare una loffa exp.

SYNONYM 5:
fare una peta exp. • (lit.): to make a fart.

SYNONYM 6:
fare una puzza exp. • (lit.): to make a stink.

SYNONYM 7:
fare una scureggia exp.

SYNONYM 8:
loffare v.

SYNONYM: 9
petare v. to fart.

SYNONYM 10:
scureggiare v.

VARIATION:
scoreggiare v.

---

fare un po'd'acqua exp. to take a leak, to urinate • (lit.): to make a little water.

example:
Scusatemi. Devo fare un salto in bagno a **fare un po'd'acqua**.

translation:
Excuse me. I need to run to the restroom **to take a leak**.

SYNONYM 1:
cambiare l'acqua al merlo/al passero *exp.* • (lit.): to change the water to the blackbird/the sparrow.

SYNONYM 2:
fare pipì *exp.* • (lit.): to make pipi.

SYNONYM 3:
pisciare *v.* • (lit.): to piss.

---

fare una cagata/cacata *exp.* to take a shit • (lit.): to make a shit.

example:
Ho mangiato così tanto che ho davvero bisogno di **fare una cagata/cacata**!

translation:
I ate so much that now I really need **to take a shit**!

SYNONYM 1:
andare di corpo *exp.* • (lit.): to go with one's body.

SYNONYM 2:
cagare/cacare *v.* • (lit.): to defecate.

SYNONYM 3:
fare la merda *exp.* • (lit.): to make shit.

SYNONYM 4:
fare la poppò/popò *exp.* (euphemism) • (lit.): to go poopoo.

fare una figura di merda
exp. to make a shitty impression, to embarrass oneself • (lit.): to make a figure of shit.

example:
Franco ieri sera **ha fatto una figura di merda** alla festa di Costanza. Ha offeso davanti a tutti la sua ex ragazza!

translation:
Last night, Franco really **made a shitty impression** at Costanza's party. He offended his ex-girlfriend in front of everyone!

SYNONYM 1:
fare una brutta/bruttissima figura *exp.* • (lit.): to make an ugly/very ugly figure.

SYNONYM 2:
fare una figura da imbecille *exp.* • (lit.): to make a figure of imbecile.

SYNONYM 3:
fare una figura da scemo/a *exp.* • (lit.): to make a figure as a stupid person.

SYNONYM 4:
fare una figura del cazzo *exp.* • (lit.): to make a figure of the penis or "dick."

---

farlo rizzare *exp.* to get it up, to make it hard, to have an erection • (lit.): to make it stand up.

example:
La prima volta che ho fatto sesso, non mi riusciva a **farlo rizzare**. Ero così nervoso!

translation:
The first time I had sex, I couldn't **get it up**. I was so nervous!

---

farsi i cazzi propri *exp.* to mind one's own business • (lit.): to make one's own dicks.

example:
Paolo non **si fa mai i cazzi suoi**. Prima o poi si caccerà in qualche guaio serio!

translation:
Paolo **never minds his own business**. Sooner or later, he's going to get in some serious trouble!

SYNONYM:
farsi gli affari propri *exp.* • (lit.): to make one's own affairs.

---

fesso/a *adj.* stupid, out of it.

example:
Credo che Antonello sia un po'**fesso**! È la quarta volta questa settimana che chiude la macchina con le chiavi dentro!

translation:
I think that Antonello is a little **out of it**! He locked his keys in his car for the fourth time this week!

VARIATION:
fessacchiotto/a *adj.*

SYNONYM 1:
coglione/a *n. & adj.*

SYNONYM 2:
minchione/a *n. & adj.* (Sicilian).

SYNONYM 3:
tonto/a *n. & adj.*

ALSO:
fare fesso qualcuno *exp.* to swindle someone • (lit.): to make someone stupid.

---

fighetta *f.* a sexy girl, a hot chick • (lit.): a cute little vagina.

example:
Voltati! Svelto! Hai visto quella bella **fighetta** che è passata davanti alla fontana? Tutti si sono fermati per guardarla. Anche il traffico si è bloccato!

translation:
Turn around! Quick! Did you see that hot **chick** who walked by the fountain? Everybody stopped to look at her. Even the traffic stopped!

NOTE:
This comes from the feminine noun *fica* or *figa*, a vulgar term for "vagina," or more closely, "pussy."

---

figlio di troia *m.* son of a bitch • (lit.): son of a sow.

example:
Armando è un **figlio di troia**! Se lo vedo gli rompo la testa!

translation:
Armando is a **son of a bitch**! If I see him, I'm going to punch his lights out!

SYNONYM 1:
figlio di maiala m. • (lit.): son of a sow.

SYNONYM 2:
figlio di puttana m. • (lit.): son of a whore.

SYNONYM 3:
figlio di zoccola m. • (lit.): son of a sewer rat.

---

finire in merda exp. to end miserably • (lit.): to end in shit.

example:
La storia fra Luigi e Sara è **finita in merda**, dopo che Sara lo ha trovato a letto con un'altra.

translation:
The relationship between Luigi and Sara **ended miserably** after Sara found him in bed with another woman.

---

fregarsene v. not to give a damn, not to give a shit.

example:
Stefano crede di poter uscire con tutte le ragazze che vuole soltanto perchè guida una Ferrari nuova di zecca. Ma io **me ne frego** della sua macchina. Preferirei uscire con Carlo, che è molto più intelligente di Stefano e anche molto più carino.

translation:
Stefano thinks that he can go out with all the girls he wants only because he drives a brand new Ferrari. But I **don't give a damn** about his car. I would rather go out with Carlo, who is much more intelligent than Stefano and also much cuter.

SYNONYM:
fottersene v. (very vulgar).

---

fuori di testa (essere) exp. to be out of one's mind • (lit.): to be out of one's head.

example:
Alessandro è uno dei più poveri fra i miei amici, ma continua a dire a tutti di essere una delle persone più ricche di Milano! Sinceramente credo che lui sia un po' **fuori di testa**.

translation:
Alessandro is one of the poorest friends I have, but he keeps telling everybody that he is one of the richest persons in Milan! Frankly I think that he is a little bit **out of his mind**.

SYNONYM 1:
non esserci con la testa exp. • (lit.): not to be there with the head.

SYNONYM 2:
partito/a (essere) adj. • (lit.): to be gone.

grassone/a *n.* a very fat man or woman, a fatso, fat slob.

example:
La mia vicina di casa è una **grassona** incredibile! Tutte le mattine la vedo agli alimentari vicino a casa nostra, a mangiarsi tre o quattro panini al salame!

translation:
Our neighbor is really a **fat slob**! Every morning I see her at the deli near our house eating three or four salami sandwiches!

SYNONYM 1:
balena *f.* • (lit.): a whale.

SYNONYM 2:
cicciobomba *n.* • (lit.): fat bomb.

SYNONYM 3:
ciccione/a *n.* • (lit.): big fat person (from the feminine noun *ciccia*, meaning "flab").

guanto *m.* condom • (lit.): glove.

example:
Oggigiorno se non ti metti il **guanto**, puoi avere guai!

translation:
Nowadays, if you don't wear a **rubber**, you could be in trouble!

SYNONYM 1:
goldone *m.* • (lit.): a gold coin that looks like a flat, unused condom.

SYNONYM 2:
impermeabile *m.* • (lit.): raincoat.

NOTE:
A common mistake made by Americans is using the term *preservativo*, thinking it means "fruit preserves." Beware that *preservativo* means "condom" in everyday slang. Therefore, if you ask your waiter or waitress for some *preservativi* with your bread, you may get a strange look!

guastafeste (un/una) *n.* a party pooper • (lit.): a party spoiler.

example:
Ieri sera eravamo tutti pronti per andare a ballare in discoteca, quando Filippo ci ha detto che non voleva accompagnarci in macchina. Filippo è proprio un **guastafeste**!

translation:
Yesterday evening we were all ready to go dancing, but Filippo told us that he didn't want to take us there in his car. Filippo is really a **party pooper**!

inculata *f.* (very vulgar) a rip-off •
(lit.): a butt-fucking.

example:
Che **inculata** ieri sera al
ristorante! Abbiamo mangiato
malissimo ed il conto era da non
crederci!

translation:
What a **rip-off** last night at the
restaurant! The food was really
awful and the bill was
unbelievable!

SYNONYM 1:
fregatura *f.* • (lit.): a rubbing.

SYNONYM 2:
inchiappettata *f.* • (lit.): to get it
between the buttocks (from the
feminine plural noun *chiappe,*
meaning "buttocks").

leccacazzi *m.* cocksucker • (lit.):
dick-licker.

example:
Il mio vicino è il più gran
leccacazzi del mondo. Ha preso
le sue chiavi ed ha scritto il suo
nome sulla fiancata della mia
macchina!

translation:
My neighbor is the biggest
cocksucker. He took his keys
and wrote his name on the side
of my car!

SYNONYM 1:
leccafave *m.* • (lit.):
"dicks-licker" from the feminine
fava, meaning "fava bean" but
used in Italian slang to mean
"penis."

SYNONYM 2:
leccauccelli *m.* • (lit.): birds-
licker (*lecca* = lick • *l'uccello* =
bird).

NOTE:
uccello *m.* dick • (lit.): bird.

leccaculo *m.* • **1.** asshole, jerk
• **2.** ass-kisser, brownnoser •
(lit.): ass-licker.

example 1:
Voi due, luridi merdosi
leccaculi! Andate via di qui o
chiamo subito la polizia!

translation:
You dirty **assholes**! Get out of
here or I'll call the police!

example 2:
Oreste è un gran **leccaculo**!
Tutte le volte che fa un viaggio
all'estero, porta un regalino al
professore di matematica.

translation:
Oreste is a big **ass-kisser**!
Every time he travels abroad, he
brings back a little present for his
math professor.

leccaculo *n.* butt-kisser, brownnoser • (lit.): ass-licker.

example:
Quella **leccaculo** di Francesca otterrà sempre ciò che vuole!

translation:
That **butt-kisser** Francesca will get anything she wants!

SYNONYM 1:
leccapiedi *m.* • (lit.): foot-licker.

SYNONYM 2:
lecchino/a *n.* • (lit.): licker.

SYNONYM 3:
ruffiano/a *n.*

---

leccapiedi *m.* brownnoser • (lit.): feet-licker.

example:
Sai come ha preso quel lavoro Gabriele? Soltanto perchè è un gran **leccapiedi** e perchè va fuori con la figlia del capo!

translation:
Do you know how Gabriele got that job? It's only because he is a big **brownnoser** and because he's dating the boss's daughter!

SYNONYM 1:
leccaculo *m.* (vulgar) • (lit.): ass-licker.

SYNONYM 2:
lecchino/a *n.* • (lit.): "a small licker."

---

leccare il culo a qualcuno *exp.* to butt kiss • (lit.): to lick someone's ass.

example:
Giacomo vuole un bel voto nel corso di filosofia e per ottenerlo non fa che **leccare il culo al professore**.

translation:
Giacomo wants a good grade in his philosophy class, and in order to get it, he does nothing but **kiss his professor's butt**.

SYNONYM 1:
fare il ruffiano/la ruffiana con qualcuno *exp.* • (lit.): to make the pimp with someone.

SYNONYM 2:
leccare i piedi a qualcuno *exp.* • (lit.): to lick someone's feet.

---

levarsi di torno *exp.* to beat it • (lit.): to move from around.

example:
Quando Silvia è stata avvicinata da quel vecchio sporcaccione, gli ha detto di lasciarla in pace e di **levarsi di torno**.

translation:
When Silvia was approached by that dirty old man, she told him to leave her alone and **beat it**.

SYNONYM 1:
alzare i tacchi *exp.* • (lit.): to lift one's heels.

SYNONYM 2:
filare *v.* • (lit.): to spin.

SYNONYM 3:
sgombrare *v.* • (lit.): to evacuate, to move out of, to vacate.

SYNONYM 4:
sloggiare *v.* • (lit.): to dislodge, to shove off, to clear out.

SYNONYM 5:
smammare *v.* (Neapolitan, from the feminine noun *mammella*, meaning "breast").

magnaccia *m.* pimp (from Roman *magnare*, a variation of the verb *mangiare*, meaning "to eat," i.e., "someone who eats with other people's money").

example:
Tutte quelle belle bionde che lavorano per il viale hanno un **magnaccia** che sta attento che loro non scappino.

translation:
All those beautiful blondes who work on the boulevard have a **pimp** who makes sure that they are not running away.

SYNONYM 1:
pappa/pappone *m.* (from the verb *pappare*, meaning "to eat").

SYNONYM 2:
protettore *m.* • (lit.): protector.

maledetta puttana *f.*
damned bitch, fucking bitch • (lit.): damned prostitute.

example:
Maledetta puttana! Con chi hai dormito ieri sera?

translation:
You **fucking bitch**! Who did you sleep with last night?

SYNONYM 1:
maledetta troia *f.* • (lit.): damned sow.

SYNONYM 2:
maledetta vacca *f.* • (lit.): damned cow.

mandare a cagare/cacare qualcuno *exp.* to tell someone to fuck off • (lit.): to send someone to shit.

example:
Quando il mio inquilino mi ha detto che non poteva pagare questo mese, l'ho **mandato a cagare**!

translation:
When my tenant told me that he could not pay me this month, I told him **to fuck off**!

SYNONYM 1:
mandare qualcuno a fanculo *exp.*

SYNONYM 2:
mandare qualcuno a fantasca *exp.* • (lit.): to send someone to do in the pocket.

SYNONYM 3:
mandare qualcuno a quel paese *exp.* • (lit.): to send someone to that country.

SYNONYM 4:
mandare qualcuno al diavolo *exp.* • (lit.): to send someone to the devil.

---

merda *f. & adj.* shit, shitty, a piece of shit, mean son of a bitch.

example:
Corrado qualche volta è davvero una **merda**; gli ho chiesto di prestarmi la sua macchina e lui ha detto no!

translation:
Sometimes Corrado is really a **shit**. I asked him if I could borrow his car and he said no!

---

merda *f.* • **1.** shit • **2.** a piece of shit (meaning "lousy") • (lit.): shit.

example 1.
Stamani, mentre camminavo sul marciapiede, ho pestato un'enorme **merda** di cane! Che puzzo!

translation:
Earlier this morning, while I was walking along the sidewalk, I stepped on a huge dog **shit**! Did it ever stink!

example 2.
Questo film è una **merda**!

translation:
This is a shitty **movie**!

EUPHEMISM 1:
cacca *m.* • (lit.): caca.

EUPHEMISM 2:
cagata *f.* • (lit.): poop.

EUPHEMISM 3:
popò *f.* • (lit.): poop, poo-poo.

"Merda!" *interj.* • (lit.): "Shit!"

example:
Merda! Ho perso l'autobus!

translation:
Shit! I missed the bus!

---

merdaio (un) *m.* a very dirty and disgusting place, a shit hole • (lit.): a place full of shit.

example:
L'appartamento di Franco e Gabriele è un **merdaio**! C'è sporco dappertutto, puzza e il bagno fa schifo!

translation:
Franco and Gabriele's apartment is a **shit hole**! It's filthy everywhere, it smells, and the bathroom is disgusting!

---

merdaiolo/a *n.* shit, despicable person, bitch.

example:
Quella **merdaiola** mi ha appena tamponato! Guarda come mi ha ridotto la macchina!

translation:
That **bitch** just rear-ended me! Look what she did to my car!

merdoso/a *adj.* a very despicable person, a shitty person, an asshole
• (lit.): a shitty one.

example:
Che **merdoso**, Giovanni! Tratta sempre male la sua ragazza quando escono insieme il fine settimana.

translation:
Giovanni is such an **asshole**! He always treats his girlfriend badly when they go out together on weekends.

SYNONYM 1:
figlio di puttana *m.* • (lit.): son of whore.

SYNONYM 2:
merda (una) *f.* • (lit.): a shit.

SYNONYM 3:
stronzo/a *n.* • (lit.): turd.

---

metterlo in culo a qualcuno *exp.* (extremely vulgar) to cheat someone, to rip someone off • (lit.): to put it in someone's ass, to buttfuck someone.

example:
La commessa di quel negozietto **me lo ha messo nel culo** ieri pomeriggio! Non mi ha dato i venti Euro di resto. Mi ha dato soltanto la metà del resto che mi doveva!

translation:
The saleswoman in that small store **cheated me** yesterday afternoon! She didn't give me the Euros back in change. She gave me only half the change she was supposed to give me!

SYNONYM 1:
fregare qualcuno *v.* • (lit.): to rub someone.

SYNONYM 2:
inculare qualcuno *v.* • (lit.): to buttfuck someone.

---

mettersi insieme *exp.* to start a serious relationship, to tie the knot.

example:
Fabrizio e Serena escono insieme soltanto da due settimane e pensano di già di **mettersi insieme**.

translation:
Fabrizio and Serena have only been going out for the past two weeks, but they are already thinking of **tying the knot**.

SYNONYM:
attaccarsi a qualcuno *exp.* • (lit.): to stick to someone.

---

mollare qualcuno *v.* to dump someone • (lit.): to let go of someone, to release someone.

example:
Francesco ha **mollato** Monica la scorsa settimana, perchè lei da poco aveva cominciato a vedersi con un altro quando Francesco era fuori città per affari.

translation:
Francesco **dumped** Monica last week because she had just recently started seeing someone else when Francesco was out of town on business.

SYNONYM:

scaricare qualcuno *exp.* to unload someone.

---

morire di/dalla noia *exp.* to die of boredom • (lit.): [same].

example:
Questa festa è veramente brutta! **Sto morendo dalla noia**! Perchè non ce ne andiamo subito?

translation:
This party is really bad! **I'm bored to death**! Why don't we get out of here right now?

---

mostrare il dito medio *exp.* to give the finger • (lit.): to show the middle finger.

example:
Ieri, mentre guidavo, qualcuno dall'autobus **mi ha mostrato il dito medio**!

translation:
Yesterday, while I was driving, someone in a bus **gave me the finger**!

NOTE:
This expression is gaining popularity in Italy because it is seen in American movies. However, the most common abusive gesture is the "cuckold gesture," especially

referring to men whose wives are unfaithful. This gesture is accomplished by raising the index and little finger symbolizing antlers. This gesture is called *fare le corna*, meaning "to do (show) the antlers."

SEE:
Gestures, *p. 154*.

noioso *adj.* boring.

example:
Mamma mia! Questa festa è così **noiosa**! Il cibo fa schifo, le ragazze sono bruttissime e la musica è insopportabile! Andiamoce!

translation:
Man! This party is so **boring**! The food is disgusting, the girls are ugly, and the music is just unbearable! Let's get out of here!

SYNONYM 1:
palla *f.* • (lit.): ball.

NOTE:
It's interesting to note that *palla* is used in the opposite way from English. In English, the expression *to have a ball* means "to have a great time." Whereas in Italian, it is used to indicate something boring.

SYNONYM 2:
palloso/a *adj.*

SYNONYM 3:
pesante *adj.* • (lit.): heavy.

SYNONYM 4:
uggioso/a *n.* (Tuscany) • (lit.): an annoying person.

pezzo di merda *m.* a despicable person, a bastard • (lit.): piece of shit.

example:
Pezzo di merda! Restituiscimi subito la borsa o chiamo la polizia e ti faccio arrestare!

translation:
You bastard! Give me back my purse right away, or I'll call the police and have you arrested!

SYNONYMS:
See – **merdoso/a**, *p. 99, 216.*

pigrone/a *n. & adj.* a lazy bum (from the masculine noun *pigro*, meaning "someone who is idle") • (lit.): big lazy bum.

example:
Mario non finisce mai i suoi lavori. Tutte le volte che può, chiede a qualcun altro di finire per lui quello che stava facendo. Che **pigrone**!

translation:
Mario never finishes his jobs. Whenever he can, he asks someone else to finish whatever he was doing. What a **lazy bum**!

SYNONYM 1:
addormentato/a *n.* (from the verb *dormire*, meaning "to sleep") • (lit.): one who sleeps (or "sleeps on the job").

SYNONYM 2:
poltrone *m.* • (lit.): someone who is very sluggish.

SYNONYM 3:
sfaticato/a *n.*

pompino *m.* blowjob • (lit.): a small pumping.

example:
Ho visto Flavia, in una macchina parcheggiata per strada, fare un **pompino** al suo ragazzo!

translation:
I saw Flavia giving a **blowjob** to her boyfriend in a car parked on the street!

SYNONYM 1:
bocchino *m.* • (lit.): cigarette holder.

SYNONYM 2:
pipa (una) *f.* • (lit.): a pipe (since it looks like the one giving the blowjob is smoking a pipe).

SYNONYM 3:
pompa (una) *f.* • (lit.): a pump.

pornazzo *m.* (from the masculine noun *porno*, meaning "pornographic movie") an X-rated movie.

example:
Hai visto? Quei due ragazzi si sono appena infilati là dentro, per vedersi un **pornazzo**!

translation:
Did you see that? Those two kids just snuck into that theater to see an **X-rated movie**!

SYNONYM: **filmaccio** *m.* a bad or dirty movie.

---

portare male gli anni *exp.* not to age well • (lit.): to bring the years badly.

example:
Francesca ha soltanto ventitré anni, ma ne dimostra quaranta! **Porta davvero male gli anni**!

translation:
Francesca is only twenty-three but she looks forty! **She really doesn't age well**!

---

prenderlo in culo da qualcuno *exp.* (very vulgar) • **1.** to get cheated, to get ripped off • **2.** to get beaten up by someone • (lit.): to get it in the ass by someone.

example:
La scorsa settimana **lo abbiamo preso nel culo** da quella concessionaria. Ci hanno venduto una macchina usata schifosa!

translation:
Last week, **we were cheated** by those car dealers. They sold us a worthless, used car!

SYNONYM 1:
farsi fregare da qualcuno *exp.*

SYNONYM 2:
farsi inculare da qualcuno *exp.* • (lit.): to get oneself butt-fucked by someone.

SYNONYM 3:
prenderlo nelle mele da qualcuno *exp.* • (lit.): to take it between the apples (meaning "buttocks").

---

prendere per il culo qualcuno *exp.* to make fun of someone, to pull someone's leg • (lit.): to get someone by the ass.

example:
Luca è un po' lento. Tutti lo **prendono per il culo** e lui nemmeno se ne accorge!

translation:
Luca is a bit slow. Everybody's **making fun of** him and he doesn't even get it!

SYNONYM 1:
fare fesso qualcuno *exp.* • (lit.): to make someone stupid.

SYNONYM 2:
prendere in giro qualcuno *exp.* • (lit.): to take someone in circle.

SYNONYM 3:
prendere qualcuno per il bavero *exp.* (Tuscan) • (lit.): to take someone by the collar.

SYNONYM 4:
prendere qualcuno per le fondelli *exp.* (Tuscan) • (lit.): to take someone from the bottoms (used to mean "buttocks").

SYNONYM 5:
prendere qualcuno per le mele *exp.* (Tuscan) • (lit.): to take someone by the apples (used to mean "buttocks").

puttana *f.* • **1.** prostitute, whore • **2.** despicable woman, bitch.

example:
Hai visto quante **puttane** ci sono per strada stasera? Ci deve essere un gran giro di sesso in questo quartiere!

translation:
Did you see how many **prostitutes** are on the street tonight? Sex must be big business in this neighborhood!

SYNONYM 1:
bagascia *f.*

SYNONYM 2:
battona *f.* • (lit.): hitter (as in "one who hits the street" from the expression *battere la strada*, meaning "to walk the streets" or more literally "to hit the street").

SYNONYM 3:
maiala *f.* • (lit.): female pig.

SYNONYM 4:
mignotta *f.* (*Rome*) • (lit.): from the French word *mignonne*, meaning "cute little woman."

SYNONYM 5:
squillo *m.* (from the verb *squillare*, meaning "to ring," i.e., call girl).

SNONYM 6:
troia *f.* • (lit.): sow.

SYNONYM 7:
zoccola *f.*

puzzare da fare schifo
exp. to stink to high heaven • (lit.): to smell/stink to disgust.

example:
Mamma mia! Questo bagno **puzza da fare schifo**! Immagino che lo puliscano soltanto una volta al mese!

translation:
Holy cow! This bathroom **smells to high heaven**! I guess they clean it only once a month!

SYNONYM:
puzzare da far vomitare
exp. • (lit.): to smell to make you vomit.

quartiere a luci rosse m.
red-light district (where prostitution takes place) • (lit.): the quarter of red lights.

example:
Se andiamo ad Amsterdam, possiamo passare per il famoso **quartiere a luci rosse** per divertirci un po'!

translation:
If we go to Amsterdam, we could stop by the famous **red-light district** to have some fun!

rompere le scatole a qualcuno exp. to annoy
someone, to tick someone off • (lit.): to break the boxes.

example:
Tutte le volte che incontro Giorgio ad una festa, lui ci prova con me, ma dopo un po', generalmente, comincia a **rompermi le scatole**.

translation:
Everytime I run into Giorgio at a party, he tries to flirt with me, but after a while he usually starts **ticking me off**.

SYNONYM 1:
rompere/scassare i coglioni exp. (vulgar) • (lit.): to break the balls.

SYNONYM 2:
rompere/scassare i marroni exp. • (lit.): to break the chestnuts.

SYNONYM 3:
rompere/scassare le palle/balle exp. • (lit.): to break the balls.

rompiscatole (un/una) n.
a pain in the neck • (lit.): box-breaker.

example:
Gianna è una gran **rompiscatole**. Tutti i giorni mi chiama dopo mezzanotte per parlarmi dei suoi problemi con Marco.

translation:
Gianna is a big **pain in the neck**. Every day, she calls me after midnight to talk to me about her problems with Marco.

SYNONYM 1:
rompi palle/balle (un/una) n. • (lit.): a ball-breaker.

SYNONYM 2:
rompicoglioni (un/una) n. • (lit.): a ball-breaker.

SYNONYM 3:
scassacazzo (un/una) n. (very vulgar) • (lit.): a dick-breaker.

schifoso/a *adj.* disgusting, gross.

example:
Queste lasagne sono **schifose**! Credo che le abbiano fatte con della carne marcia!

translation:
This lasagna is **disgusting**! I think they made it with rotten meat!

SYNONYM:
da fare vomitare *exp.* enough to make you throw up • (lit.): vomit-making.

VARIATION:
da fare schifo *exp.* to be disgusting, gross • *Questa pasta è salata da fare schifo; This pasta is disgustingly salty!*

sciolta (la) *f.* the runs, diarrhea • (lit.): the melted.

example:
Tommaso ha mangiato dieci chili di prugne ed ora ha **la sciolta**!

translation:
Tommaso ate twenty pounds of prunes and now he has got **the runs**!

SYNONYM:
cacarella *f.* • (lit.): the shits (from the verb *cacare*, meaning "to shit").

scopata facile *f.* an easy lay (from the verb *scopare*, meaning "to sweep") • (lit.): an easy sweep.

example:
Soltanto perchè Tiziana è bella ed amichevole, i ragazzi presumono che sia una **scopata facile**.

translation:
Just because Tiziana is beautiful and friendly, guys just assume she's an **easy lay**.

NOTE:
The feminine noun *scopata* comes from the verb *scopare*, literally meaning "to sweep," yet is commonly used in Italian slang to mean "to have sex" and is considered very vulgar.

spettegolare *v.* to gossip • (lit.): to tattle.

example:
Serena non fa altro che **spettegolare**. Tutti nel rione, per colpa sua, pensano che mia sorella esca con tre ragazzi diversi. Ma non è vero!

translation:
Serena does nothing but **gossip**. Because of that, everyone in the neighborhood thinks my sister goes out with three different guys. But it's not true!

SYNONYM 1:
chiacchierare *v.* • (lit.): to chatter, to blab, to gossip.

SYNONYM 2:
dire male *exp.* • (lit.): to say bad.

SYNONYM 3:
mormorare *v.* • (lit.): to babble, to grumble.

---

stitico/a *adj.* • **1.** constipated • **2.** stingy, tight with one's money.

example 1:
Mario non mangia verdure da sei mesi! Probabilmente è **stitico**!

translation:
Mario hasn't eaten vegetables for the past six months! He's probably **constipated**!

example 2:
Mio nonno, quando vado a trovarlo, non mi dà mai soldi per compare un gelato. È davvero **stitico**!

translation:
Whenever I visit my grandfather, he never gives me any money to buy ice cream. He's really **tight with money**!

---

tappo *m.* a very short guy • (lit.): cork.

example:
Due giorni fa, mentre bevevo un caffè al bar, un brutto **tappo** ha versato tutto il suo cappuccino sulla mia gonna!

translation:
Two days ago, while I was having a coffee at the bar, an ugly **runt** spilled all his cappuccino on my skirt!

VARIATION 1:
tappetto *m.*

VARIATION 2:
tappino *m.* • (lit.): small cork.

SYNONYM 1:
mezza cartuccia (una) *f.* • (lit.): half a cartridge.

SYNONYM 2:
mezza sega (una) *f.* • (lit.): half a saw.

---

testa di cazzo *f.* a despicable person, an asshole• (lit.): dickhead.

example:
Simone è una **testa di cazzo**! Guida sempre come un pazzo, e uno di questi giorni la polizia lo fermerà e gli farà una multa pazzesca!

translation:
Simone is an **asshole**! He always drives like a mad person, and one of these days the police are going to stop him and give him a huge ticket!

SYNONYM 1:
coglione/a *n.* • (lit.): testicle.

SYNONYM 2:
cretino/a *n.* • (lit.): cretin.

SYNONYM 3:
fava *m.* • (lit.): fava bean.

SYNONYM 4:
imbecille n. & adj. • (lit.):
imbecile.

---

testona pelata f. a bald guy, a
"baldy" • (lit.): big peeled head.

example:
Non riesco a credere che Cinzia sia
fidanzata con quell' orribile **crapa
pelata**! Lui non ha un briciolo di
classe e la tratta come se fosse la
sua donna di servizio.

translation:
I cannot believe that Cinzia is
engaged to that ugly **bald guy**!
He doesn't have an iota of class at
all and treats her as if she were his
servant.

SYNONYM:
zucca pelata f. • (lit.): peeled
pumpkin.

---

testone/a di merda n. a fucking
idiot • (lit.): big head of shit.

example:
Marco è un gran **testone di
merda**. È sempre nei guai e non
mi dà mai retta.

translation:
Marco is a **fucking idiot**. He's
always in trouble and never follows
my advise.

SYNONYM 1:
fessacchione/a n. • (lit.): big
idiot.

SYNONYM 2:
imbecillone/a n. • (lit.): big
imbecile.

SYNONYM 3:
stronzone/a n. • (lit.): big turd.

SYNONYM 4:
stupidone/a n. • (lit.): big
idiot.

**tirare un bidone a
qualcuno** exp. to stand
someone up on a date or
appointment • (lit.): to throw a
trash can at someone.

example:
Marco sarebbe dovuto passare a
prendermi alle 10:00 per andare
al locale, ma non si è mai fatto
vedere. Questa volta mi ha
davvero **tirato un bidone**!

translation:
Marco was supposed to pick me
up at 10:00 to go to the club, but
he never showed up. He really
stood me up this time!

VARIATION 1: **bidonare
qualcuno** v.

VARIATION 2:
fare un bidone a qualcuno
exp. • (lit.): to make a trash can.

---

tirato/a adj. stingy • (lit):
pulled.

example:
Giordano è sempre molto
tirato. Anche quando esce con
la sua ragazza, non paga mai il
conto al ristorante.

translation:
Giordano is always very **stingy**. Even when he goes out with his girlfriend, he never pays the bill at the restaurant.

NOTE:
You'll notice in the opening that *tirato da morire* was used. *Da morire* is a common Italian expression, meaning "extremely" or "big-time."

SYNONYM 1:
spilorcio/a *adj.*

SYNONYM 2:
taccagno/a *adj.*

SYNONYM 3:
tirchio/a *adj.*

---

troia *f.* prostitute • (lit.): sow.

example:
Ieri sera Giacomo è andato con una **troia** bellissima e molto giovane.

translation:
Last night, Giacomo took off with a beautiful and very young **prostitute**.

SYNONYMS:
See – **puttana**, p. 70, 220.

---

troiaio *m.* a very dirty, filthy place • (lit): pigsty.

example:
Il nuovo appartamento di Federico è un **troiaio**! I muri sono sporchi e c'è un gran puzzo di uova marce!

translation:
Federico's new apartment looks like a **pigsty**! The walls are dirty and there's a terrible stench of rotten eggs!

SYNONYM 1:
maialaio *m.* • (lit.): pigsty.

SYNONYM 2:
porcaio *m.* • (lit.): pigsty.

"Va'a farti fottere!" *interj.*
"Fuck you!" • (lit.): "Go get yourself fucked!"

example:
Va'a farti fottere! Brutto bastardo! Rendimi la borsa!

translation:
Fuck off! Ugly bastard! Give my purse back to me!

SYNONYM 1:
"Va'a cagare!" *interj.* • (lit.): "Go shit!"

SYNONYM 2:
"Va'a prendertelo in culo!" *interj.* • (lit.): "Go get it in your ass!"

SYNONYM 3:
"Vaffantasca!" *interj.* (Tuscan) • (lit.): "Go do in the pocket!"

"Va'al diavolo!" *interj*. "Go to hell!" • (lit.): "Go to the Devil!"

example:
Va'al diavolo, vecchio maiale! Lasciami stare!

translation:
Go to hell, you dirty old man! Leave me alone!

SYNONYM:
"Va'alla/in malora!" *interj*. • (lit.): "Go to the/in devil!"

"Vaffanculo!" *interj*. "Fuck off!" "Fuck you!" • (lit.): "Go do in the ass!" (short for *"Va'a fare in culo!"*).

example:
Ehi! **Vaffanculo**! Quel posto è mio! Se non te ne vai subito esco di macchina e te le do!

translation:
Hey, you! **Fuck off**! That was my spot! If you don't leave right away, I'm going to get out of my car and kick your butt!

vecchio sporcaccione *m*. dirty old man.

example:
Il nonno di Simona è davvero un **vecchio sporcaccione**. Tutte le volte che vede una ragazza sull'autobus, le si avvicina e le tocca il sedere!

translation:
Simona's grandfather is really a **dirty old man**. Every time he sees a cute girl on the bus, he moves close to her and touches her butt!

SYNONYM 1:
vecchio maiale *m*. • (lit.): old pig, swine, hog.

SYNONYM 2:
vecchio porco *m*. • (lit.): old pig, swine, hog.

SYNONYM 3: **vecchio schifoso** *m*. • (lit.): disgusting old man.

vomitare l'anima *exp*. to throw up, to barf one's guts up • (lit.): to vomit one's soul.

example:
Tutte le volte che torno a casa dopo aver mangiato a casa di Luca, **vomito l'anima mia**!

translation:
Every time I come back home after having eaten at Luca's, **I barf my guts up**!

SYNONYM:
fare i gattini • (lit.): to make the kittens.

zucca pelata *f.* a bald person, baldy • (lit.): a peeled pumpkin.

example:

Di'a quella **zucca pelata** che non ha bisogno di andare dal barbiere!

translation:

Tell that **bald guy** he doesn't need a barber!

SYNONYM 1:

rapato/a *adj.* • (lit.): from the verb *rapare*, meaning "to crop" or "to shave."

SYNONYM 2:

tosato/a *adj.* • (lit.): from the verb *tosare*, meaning "to shear" or "to clip."

ORDER FORM

SLANGMAN PUBLISHING

12206 Hillslope Street
Studio City, CA 91604 • USA

INTERNATIONAL:
1-818-769-1914

TOLL FREE (US/Canada):
1-877-SLANGMAN
(1-877-752-6462)

Worldwide FAX:
1-413-647-1589

Get the latest news, preview chapters, and shop online at:

WWW.SLANGMAN.COM

SHIPPING

Domestic Orders

SURFACE MAIL
(delivery time 5-7 days).
Add $5 shipping/handling for the first item, $1 for each additional item.

RUSH SERVICE
available at extra charge. Please telephone us for details.

International Orders

OVERSEAS SURFACE
(delivery time 6-8 weeks).
Add $5 shipping/handling for the first item, $2 for each additional item. Note that shipping to some countries may be more expensive. Please contact us for details.

OVERSEAS AIRMAIL
available at extra charge. Please phone for details.

PRODUCT	TYPE	PRICE	QTY	TOTAL
AMERICAN SLANG & IDIOMS				
STREET SPEAK 1: *Complete Course in American Slang & Idioms*	book	$18.95		
	cassette	$12.50		
STREET SPEAK 2: *Complete Course in American Slang & Idioms*	book	$21.95		
	cassette	$12.50		
STREET SPEAK 3: *Complete Course in American Slang & Idioms*	book	$21.95		
	cassette	$12.50		
SPANISH SLANG & IDIOMS				
STREET SPANISH 1: *The Best of Spanish Slang*	book	$16.95		
	cassette	$12.50		
STREET SPANISH 2: *The Best of Spanish Idioms*	book	$16.95		
	cassette	$12.50		
STREET SPANISH 3: *The Best of Naughty Spanish*	book	$16.95		
	cassette	$12.50		
STREET SPANISH DICTIONARY & THESAURUS	book	$16.95		
FRENCH SLANG & IDIOMS				
STREET FRENCH 1: *The Best of French Slang*	book	$16.95		
	cassette	$12.50		
STREET FRENCH 2: *The Best of French Idioms*	book	$16.95		
	cassette	$12.50		
STREET FRENCH 3: *The Best of Naughty French*	book	$16.95		
	cassette	$12.50		
STREET FRENCH DICTIONARY & THESAURUS	book	$16.95		
ITALIAN SLANG & IDIOMS				
STREET ITALIAN 1: *The Best of Italian Slang*	book	$16.95		
	cassette	$12.50		
STREET ITALIAN 2: *The Best of Naughty Italian*	book	$16.95		
	cassette	$12.50		

Total for Merchandise	
Sales Tax *(California Residents Only add current sales tax %)*	
Shipping *(See Left)*	
ORDER TOTAL	

prices subject to change

Name _____

(School/Company) _____

Street Address _____

City _____ State/Province _____ Postal Code _____

Country _____ Phone _____ Email _____

METHOD OF PAYMENT (CHECK ONE)

☐ Personal Check or Money Order *(Must be in U.S. funds and drawn on a U.S. bank.)*

☐ VISA   ☐ Master Card   ☐ Discover

Credit Card Number

Expiration Date

⬆ **Signature** *(important!)*

PLEASE SEE ORDER FORM ON OTHER SIDE!